W9-CQO-774

Gary Wakat

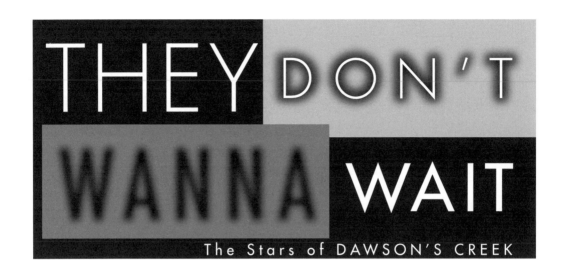

THEY DON'T WANNA WAIT

The Stars of DAWSON'S CREEK

KATHË TIBBS &
BIFF L. PETERSON

ECW PRESS

Copyright © ECW PRESS, 1999

All rights reserved. No part of this publication may be
reproduced, stored in a retrieval system, or transmitted
in any form by any process — electronic, mechanical,
photocopying, recording, or otherwise — without
the prior written permission of ECW PRESS.

CANADIAN CATALOGUING IN PUBLICATION DATA
Tibbs, Kathë
They don't wanna wait : the stars of Dawson's Creek

ISBN 1-55022-389-5

1. Dawson's Creek (Television program). 2. Television actors and actresses — United
States — Biography. I. Peterson, Biff L. II. Title. III. Title: They don't want to wait.

PN1992.77.D36T52 1999   791.45′72   C99-931990-6

Cover design by Tania Craan
Layout by Mary Bowness
Printed by Printcrafters

Distributed in Canada by General Distribution Services,
325 Humber Blvd., Etobicoke, Ontario M9W 7C3

Distributed in the United States by LPC Group-InBook,
1436 West Randolph Street, Chicago, Illinois, USA 60607

Published by ECW PRESS
2120 Queen Street East, Suite 200,
Toronto, Ontario, M4E 1E2
www.ecw.ca/press

The publication of *They Don't Wanna Wait* has been generously supported by
The Canada Council, the Ontario Arts Council, and the Government of Canada
through the Book Publishing Industry Development Program. **Canada**

TABLE OF
CONTENTS

ACKNOWLEDGMENTS

Biff L. Peterson would like to extend a tremendous thanks to Tracy Weaver for her research assistance. Thanks also to Jack David and Jennifer Hale at ECW Press, Joal Ryan, Marmoset Man, Dili "Deal" Munky, and everyone at End of the World Enterprises.

Kathë Tibbs would like to thank Rachel Jones, Jen Hale, Jack David, Mary Bowness, Sally Catto, Stefanie and Jolene Bond, Michael Holmes, Chad Wallace, and the Laws: Marlyn, Derrick, and Sacha.

PROLOGUE

Back in January 1998, when 15-year-old blond bombshell Jen Lindley pulled up in front of her grandparents' house and strode out of the car in that terrific slow-motion shot, she did far more than simply distract young Dawson Leery's faithful eye from his best friend and latent love interest, Joey Potter. She helped change the way American teenagers watch prime-time television.

Since the dawn of the television age, the boob tube has attempted to portray the struggles of adolescence but, because of network standards and practices, social mores, and the overriding fact that the shows were written by out-of-touch adults, it usually failed to present anything beyond mere pablum. In the 1950s and 60s, shows like *Ozzie and Harriet*, *Father Knows Best*, and *My Three Sons* showed teens turning to their strong, upstanding parents for help, overcoming such coming-of-age obstacles as bullies, first dates, and bad kids who cheat on their math tests. The 1970s brought with it shows like *Family Affair*, *The Brady Bunch*, *The Partridge Family*, and Aaron Spelling's *Family*, in which issues like divorce, family dysfunction, and sibling rivalry were discussed but inevitably washed over. And then came shows like

Welcome Back, Kotter and *21 Jump Street*, where inner-city kids faced problems such as racism, drugs, and violence, but a caring teacher or cop usually had the answers. All the interesting stuff that happens in real life — like sex, infidelity, drugs, suicide, rage — were left to the rich white folks on prime-time soap operas like *Dallas* and *Dynasty*.

In the early 1990s, the then-fledgling Fox network changed the course of television history when it introduced *Beverly Hills, 90210*, which grafted the *Knots Landing*–type formula onto the Clearasil-age landscape, substituting a group of slutty privileged high school students for those other shows' slutty privileged adults. Never before had audiences watched teen characters living their lives so brazenly — they fell in love, had sex, dumped one another, cheated, became alcoholics, passed out — it was magic. Then, a few years later, the Warner Brothers Network premiered *Party of Five*, a more subdued drama about five angst-ridden teen siblings growing into adulthood together after their parents' death.

The inspiration for *Dawson's Creek* lies somewhere between the racy *Beverly Hills, 90210* and the heart-heavy *Party of Five* — and somewhere else altogether. What sets *Creek* apart from everything that preceded it is its theme of lost innocence and its recognition that today's teens are mature enough to handle it, even at their semi-tender age. A decade ago, it might have been risqué for one of those Generation X kids on *90210* to get an earring or — God forbid! — a nose ring, but for today's Generation Y crowd (or Generation Next, or any one of several other catch-phrases), body piercings are pedestrian unless complemented by ample tattoos. Today, the Internet makes international news or necrophilic smut equally accessible to small kids, high-schoolers storm onto their campuses with AK-47's and blast away their teachers and classmates, and so on. Dawson's circle of friends, and the situations they find themselves in each week, may be self-absorbed and fatalistic at times, but their world in tiny Capeside, Massachusetts, is a hyper-real microcosm of the actual reality in teen America today. Young viewers who have made *Dawson's Creek* their number-one rated show undoubtedly recognize this. They also identify with Dawson Leery, the idealist, who's always trying to fathom the changes swirling around him. And, of course, the audience (particularly girls) loves the stars of the show, who are attractive, articulate, and, according to their publicists, still unhitched.

This is the story of *Dawson's Creek*, the show whose debut was the flashpoint of a teen revolution in television, movies, and other media and helped ignite a post-pubescent boom in Hollywood — a boom that has seen young actors with relatively little professional experience, like *Creek* heartthrob James Van Der Beek, suddenly top-billed in major motion pictures. It's not just about the show itself, with its photogenic characters, frank dialogue, and sexually charged coming-of-age drama, but also a behind-the-scenes look at the market forces that created the modern youth-centric TV program phenomenon, the thirtysomething writer who reinvented teen TV and movies by revisiting his own past, and the talented young actors and actresses who bring the show to life and have become major stars virtually overnight. It is also an appreciation of the truths that the show reveals each week about love, friendship, loss, and trust — truths that Dawson, Joey, Pacey, Jen, and the rest strive to understand, even if it means losing their already fast-fading innocence. Like the song says, they don't wanna wait.

THE CAST OF
DAWSON'S CREEK

CREEK GOD
JAMES VAN DER BEEK
(DAWSON LEERY)

BIRTHDATE: March 8, 1977
BIRTHPLACE: Cheshire, Connecticut
EDUCATION: Drew University (Madison, New Jersey; majoring in English, minoring in Sociology; studies suspended)
STATS: Height: 6′; Eyes: Brown; Hair: Brown

When Kevin Williamson suggested to WB Network executives that they cast an absolute nobody named James Van Der Beek in the lead role of their new teen drama, they balked at first. "It's gotta be this kid!" Williamson reportedly screamed, "Nobody knows the character better than me, because it *is* me!" As everyone knows by now, Dawson is Williamson's alter-ego, and as portrayed by the forthright, handsome young actor from Connecticut, he represents not what Williamson was really like at 15 years old, but the ideal kid he wishes he *could* have been.

It may be nothing more than the publicity machine at

work, but it seems there are some spooky similarities between Dawson and his counterpart Van Der Beek. Dawson adorns his walls with Steven Spielberg movie posters; Van Der Beek says posters for *The Fantasticks*, *Jesus Christ Superstar*, and other Broadway plays hung on his own bedroom walls. Dawson constantly searches for meaning and rationalizes everything, but it is his irrational hormones that make his life interesting; in the same vein, Van Der Beek says he thinks kids watch *Dawson's Creek* because it portrays teens in an intelligent light, not because it's filled with sexual tension and open discussions about doing the wild thang.

"What I get is people coming up to me and saying, 'you guys talk the way we feel. I wish I could process these emotions and verbalize them the way you guys do,'" Van Der Beek said in an *US* magazine interview. "What's striking a chord with fans of the show is that they're not condescended to." Still, Van Der Beek acknowledges that sex is a viewer magnet, and he's a little miffed that it has brought a certain level of disrepute to the show among the older set. "There are critics who say, 'these kids have too much sex on the brain,'" he added. "But those people are in some serious denial. They better sit down and have a talk with their own kids. They don't think their kids are thinking about this stuff? That scares me."

Described by those who know him as an old-school, Jimmy Stewart–type gentleman who addresses people with "sir" and "ma'am," James Van Der Beek became an actor at age 13, while attending private Cheshire Academy High School on full scholarship, in his hometown of Cheshire, Connecticut. After suffering a concussion while trying to catch a pass in football, Van Der Beek was ordered by his doctor to give up the sport for a year. Sidelined and bored, he turned his attention from the gridiron to the stage and was cast as Danny Zuko in a local production of *Grease*. He did community

James Van Der Beek as a senior in high school.

theater for three years, then asked his parents for permission to audition for professional acting gigs in New York. Van Der Beek's mom, a former Broad-way dancer, joined him on the train ride to the Big Apple where, in just one day, he found a manager and an agent; he was still a junior in high school.

In 1994, his professional thespian career crawled out of the starting gate. He was cast as Fergus, a young idealist in an off-Broadway production of Pulitzer Prize–winning playwright Edward Albee's *Finding the Sun*, before returning to Connecticut for a run of *Shenandoah* at the Goodspeed Opera House. In 1995, Van Der Beek landed a bit role on the soap opera *As the World Turns*, and he worked in his first feature film, *Angus*, playing Rick Sanford, a bullying jock; the film is the story of a nerdy, fat high school student who takes revenge on his classmates after they elect him prom king as a practical joke. Van Der Beek's role in the film was substantial, but the movie dive-bombed at the box office and did nothing for his career. However, his shooting schedule required him to miss a lot of school and he was impeached from his recently elected position of class vice-president at Cheshire Academy. Van Der Beek appeared in another movie, *I Love You, I Love You Not* (1996, starring Jeanne Moreau and Claire Danes), a wistful tale of love and Jewish persecution, playing Tony — a role Van Der Beek describes as a "neo-Nazi slimeball."

Although he now had two features on his résumé, instead of heading west for Hollywood, Van Der Beek enrolled at Drew University in New Jersey and lived the student life for two years, as his acting career seemed to have fizzled. Never having been a popular kid in high school, he found himself making up lost ground and "regressing" in college, concentrating on his socializing and partying rather than his studies. He regretfully admits that, even though his grades were good, he was often snow-jobbing his English professors,

James on the set of *Varsity Blues*.

faking his assignments. "I wrote papers on books I never read," he told *Seventeen* magazine in 1999. "How'd I get away with it? Basically I'm just a really good bullshitter. I've found that people who actually read the [assigned] book end up writing something that the professor has already read a million times. Someone who hasn't read the book has to get really creative and turn in something the professor has never seen, so you get a better grade." Van Der Beek's academic fakery must have been legendary: according to some reports, he was placed on the Dean's list at least once.

But college studies were put on hold when, in April 1997, Van Der Beek landed an audition for *Dawson's Creek*. It wasn't exactly a slam-dunk on the young actor's part. "He [Van Der Beek] was really nervous, and it showed," Kevin Williamson told *People* in 1998. But, after a shaky first reading, "he came back into the room and stunned us. We knew he was Dawson. He's very bright, but he's also very vulnerable. I like that, because it keeps him 15 years old."

Well, to be fair, almost no one out there in viewerland would believe that that this square-jawed, well-dressed, killer-haired, and well-spoken man is a 15-year-old high school student; after all, how many 15-year-olds hold such articulate, literate philosophy sessions amongst themselves, like Dawson's gang, on a regular basis? Van Der Beek attributes his own affinity for (and identification with) the Dawson character with helping the audience suspend such disbelief: "Dawson and I were very impassioned at an early age. He's a burgeoning filmmaker whose idealism sometimes makes him oblivious. He's a bit of an innocent, and is frequently off in his own little world, all of which I can definitely relate to," he told *People*.

Age difference aside, Van Der Beek has become a classic-style teen idol, with thousands of girls flocking to his rare promotional appearances in hopes of flinging their under-garments at him. His star is rising fast, more so than any other *Dawson's Creek* personality, and perhaps more so than any other male star of his young generation. In 1998, Van Der Beek was named one of *People* magazine's 50 Most Beautiful People, and his inevitable movie career was jump-started with the college football drama *Varsity Blues* (released early 1999), which starred Jon Voight and Scott Caan (son of James). In the film, Van Der Beek plays John "Mox" Moxon, a cerebral second-string quarterback who reads literature while warming the bench for the Coyotes of West Canaan, Texas. In this overblown, youth-versus-the-older-generation tale, Moxon is at constant odds with the tyrannical football coach Bud Kilmer (Voight), especially when the star quarterback goes down with an injury and Mox becomes the main man. During the quintessential "big game," the coach wigs out and Mox must lead the team to victory — the kids symbolically leave the nest, no longer needing the oldies to mentor them.

James holds up his MTV Movie Award for Best Breakthrough
Performance — Male.

Despite tepid critical reviews, *Varsity Blues* was a moderate hit, making an impressive $32 million in its first two weeks of release and maintaining the No. 1 spot at the box office during that period. Studio officials attributed this success partly to the fact that Van Der Beek received top billing in the advertising campaign. "[Van Der Beek] has proven once and for all that he has the goods," Paul Schulman, an ad buyer for Paramount, which released the film, told *USA Today*. For his part, Van Der Beek said he hoped the film would open up other acting possibilities for him, but he expressed no desire to do a David Caruso and leave *Dawson's Creek* at the height of its popularity. "Honestly, right now, being in a television show offers a tremendous amount of security," he told *USA Today*. "Even if *Varsity Blues* was a flop, I was still going to have a job. I'm locked in on the show for three or four more years, and I'll stay as long as they'll keep me."

By all accounts, James Van Der Beek is going to be a star for a while to come. Luckily, perhaps, his early acting struggles have fostered a deep appreciation for his immense, seemingly immediate success. So far, there's no sign it's all gone to his head. "I mean, two years ago I was in college and now I have this job and everything's different," he told *Seventeen* magazine in 1999. "It's hard to try to wrap your mind around it."

JAMES VAN DER BEEK FILMOGRAPHY

Films: *Angus* (1995, Rick Sanford); *I Love You, I Love You Not* (1996, Tony); *Varsity Blues* (1999, John "Mox" Moxon); *Harvest* (1999*); *Castle in the Sky* (1999, voice of Patzu); *Texas Rangers* (2000).

*Note: *Harvest* was reportedly filmed circa 1996–97, prior to *Dawson's Creek*; Van Der Beek's subsequent popularity has generated interest in the film among distributors and it was reportedly to be released in 1999.

ON-AGAIN, OFF-AGAIN GIRLFRIEND
KATIE HOLMES
(JOSEPHINE "JOEY" POTTER)

BIRTHDATE: December 18, 1978
BIRTHPLACE: Toledo, Ohio
EDUCATION: Notre Dame Academy (Toledo, Ohio); accepted to Columbia University (New York, New York)
STATS: Height: 5'8"; Eyes: Brown; Hair: Brown

When *Dawson's Creek* premiered in January 1998, its cast members had varying degrees of experience on stage and screen. And Katie Noelle Holmes, cast as Dawson Leery's doe-eyed, girl-next-doorish best friend/love interest, probably had the least experience of them all. Just two years before, she was a normal teen in Toledo, Ohio, a junior in high school whose acting was limited to the school stage. But her lack of real-world savvy may have been the very trait that the *Dawson's Creek* creators were looking for when casting the role of Joey, a strong-willed, street-smart-on-the-surface (yet inexperienced and naïve underneath) young teen.

"My original choice for the role of Joey was Selma (*Cruel Intentions*) Blair, but I felt it was my duty to go through the videos other young actresses had submitted," Kevin Williamson told the *Ottawa Sun* newspaper in 1999. Among those videos was the same tape that had won Katie Holmes an audition — and later a role — in Ang Lee's 1997 film *The Ice Storm*. The tape was recorded at her home, and her mother was reading another character's lines, "Here was this little girl in her family's rumpus room staring at the camera with her mom reading the boy's lines off-camera," Williamson said. "In just a few seconds she had me mesmerized. I not only knew I'd found my Joey but I knew I was seeing a star in the making."

In just a little more than two years, Katie Holmes went from being a total unknown from the Midwest to one of the hottest young actresses in Hollywood; from a high school drama student to a major role in *Go*, one of the hippest films of 1998 (made by *Swingers* director Doug Liman); she went from conservative Catholic schoolgirl to ripping off most of her clothes (sorry, though, no nudity) in Williamson's first film as director, *Teaching Mrs. Tingle*, in which she was top-billed; *and* she has become one of Williamson's closest pals, frequently crashing at his home when she's in L.A. — ensuring that she'll be hot in Hollywood as long as he is, if not longer.

The story of Holmes' career so far is one of those dream-come-true fairy tales that are hard to believe; it is also exemplary of how Williamson and the other *Dawson's Creek* creators were willing to venture into unknown territory and seek out unfamiliar faces to assemble their ideal ensemble. It all began in the summer of 1996, when Holmes was 17, and when she went to New York to attend a modeling convention. A Los Angeles talent agent spotted her and convinced her parents (her father, Marty Holmes, is a lawyer; her mom, Kathleen, is a homemaker) to let him represent her. Her Catholic father wasn't ecstatic about the idea: "I think we had all of Toledo convincing my dad to let me go," she later told *us* magazine. Then Holmes and her mom flew to Los Angeles for what was supposed to be a six-week-long stint auditioning for television pilots; this was cut short, however, when Holmes nailed her very first audition and won a small role in *The Ice Storm*. This critically acclaimed, yet somewhat overlooked film is a sort of *Big Chill* set in well-to-do New Canaan, Connecticut, during the early 1970s; the story, which focuses on two families involved in wife-swapping, drugs, and other misguided travails, is a serious examination of love, sex, and family issues in a world of decaying values. A 16-year-old prep

Katie goofs around for her high school yearbook.

school student (Tobey Maguire) comes home for Thanks-giving, but then escapes his parents' dysfunctional world and heads south to Manhattan for a romantic evening with a rich coed he's obsessed with (played by Holmes); in a darkly funny scene, Maguire plies Holmes with pills and booze to make her more receptive to his advances; instead, she passes out in the living room. This aspect of the script caused some strain in Holmes' conservative household: when her mother read *The Ice Storm*'s script, with its wife-swapping and pot smoking, she reportedly broke into tears and almost wanted to take her daughter out of the movie.

Rather than stay in Los Angeles and continue working after completing *The Ice Storm*, Holmes returned to Toledo to finish her senior year at her all-girls Catholic high school, but her agent in California kept sending out that videotape. More TV pilot auditions were approaching, and scripts were forwarded to Ohio for her to read; one of those scripts she received was for a show called *Dawson's Creek*. After watching Holmes' audition tape, Kevin Williamson wanted her to fly to Hollywood so she could meet with him and the WB Network executives, but Holmes declined — she was starring as Lola in a local production of *Damn Yankees*, and the play opened on the day that Williamson wanted her to jump on a plane. "I said I couldn't possibly get to L.A. for a week," she recalled in an *Ottawa Sun* interview. "I needed to complete the run of the play." Luckily, Williamson was able to convince the WB officials that Holmes was worth waiting for, and she got the part.

Fans of *Dawson's Creek* seem to have a love-hate affinity for Joey Potter; they want her and Dawson to finally get it over with, get together and get it on; yet they're driven mad by her overly analytical streak. They appreciate Joey's strength of character but they get frustrated with her naïveté, such as when she turns a blind's eye to all the incriminating evidence suggesting her father is involved with drugs. And they get sick of her blaming that hottie Jen Lindley for sweeping Dawson away; after all, a man's a man, even if he's only 15 years old. And, even though she's the second-youngest of the six principal *Creek* cast members, Holmes noted in a 1999 interview with *E! Online* that it's no cinch to capture that adolescent confusion when you're a 20-year-old actress playing a pubescent kid. "It's going to be hard to go back to playing a 15-year-old . . . Joey tries to be older and wise, but she's lacking in the experience department." As for Joey's soapy on-off relationship with Dawson, Holmes noted that sometimes the fans take it too personally. "Any time I break up with Dawson or question him, viewers turn against me. I think we'll probably make up again, and hopefully they'll understand," she said.

Of the four principal *Dawson's Creek* players, Katie Holmes has used the show's immense popularity as a springboard to a film career to the greatest extent. She was the first to cash in on the show's cachet with a co-starring role in *Disturbing Behavior*, which was released in the summer of 1998, just a few months after *Dawson's Creek* premiered. The film, directed by *X-Files* veteran David Nutter, was one of several teens-in-peril movies that came out after the successful *Scream* movies and attempted to mimic the Williamsonesque formula, but failed miserably. The film was described by one reviewer as "*The Stepford Teens* with a touch of *Invasion of the Body Snatchers*, *Heathers* and *A Clockwork Orange*," and, like *Scream*, it was supposed to be both scary and funny but in the end was neither. For her role as Rachel Wagner, Holmes was given an image makeover that included piercings and studs — quite a stretch from the girl-next-door type she's usually known as, and once again her parents cringed. "Oh my God, it was terrible," her father told *Rolling Stone* magazine. "All I

Katie's senior class photo.

was thinking about is, if the nuns saw her now, oh my gosh."

Despite her role in *Disturbing Behavior*, Holmes has mostly avoided the type of low-budget, big-box-office teen horror movies with which many of her peers (Sarah Michelle Gellar, Jennifer Love Hewitt, Neve Campbell) have forged their movie careers. Holmes' next film, in which she co-starred as part of a great ensemble cast, was the vastly underrated dark comedy *Go* (released April 1999). Directed by Doug Liman, whose *Swingers* (1996) helped fuel the retro-lounge music craze, this film, with its adventures in underground drug culture, swinging sex, pyramid schemes, topless bars, and self-inflicted wounds, surely disturbed Holmes' parents even more than *The Ice Storm*.

And then, in only her fourth feature film (not counting *Muppets from Space*, in which she made a cameo appearance), Holmes was thrust front-and-center as Leigh Ann, the would-be valedictorian who refuses to take a mediocre grade from her history teacher lying down, in *Teaching Mrs. Tingle*. In the latter two films, Holmes began to show real promise as a big-screen actress, although it must be noted that neither *Go* nor *Teaching Mrs. Tingle* appeared to tap her full range of acting abilities; in *Tingle*, for example, Holmes' character is mostly dull compared to the more wide-ranging part played by Marisa Coughlin, who tends to upstage Holmes whenever they're onscreen together. Still, the roles keep coming. Holmes next starred in *Wonder Boys* (1999, based on the novel by Michael Chabon) as Hannah Green, a college freshman with a crush on a teacher (Michael Douglas), who's going through a mid-life crisis and doesn't reciprocate her feelings. The film also stars Holmes' *Ice Storm* buddy, Tobey Maguire.

While *Dawson's Creek* is filming, Holmes now lives alone in a Wilmington, North Carolina, apartment and hangs around with the other cast members at a restaurant called

Vinnie's or at Van Der Beek and Jackson's bachelor pad. She was accepted to Columbia University but has deferred her enrollment until her duties to *Dawson's Creek* are fulfilled. And, then, she just might take a hiatus from showbiz to complete her education. "I'm contractually obligated and emotionally attached to *Dawson's*," she told *E! Online*. "It's something I definitely want to continue doing. But I also want to be a well-educated person. I think I deserve that. [Education is] not something I look upon lightly."

KATIE HOLMES FILMOGRAPHY

The Ice Storm (1997, Libbets Casey); *Disturbing Behavior* (1998, Rachel Wagner); *Go* (1999, Claire Montgomery); *Muppets from Space* (1999, herself); *Teaching Mrs. Tingle* (1999, Leigh Ann Prescott); *Wonder Boys* (1999, Hannah Green).

HOT LOINS, SMARTASS

JOSHUA JACKSON
(PACEY WITTER)

BIRTHDATE: June 11, 1978

BIRTHPLACE: Vancouver, British Columbia

EDUCATION: Kitsilano High School (Vancouver, British Columbia); University of British Columbia (deferred)

STATS: Height: 6'; Eyes: Green; Hair: Brown

If Dawson Leery is the hero of *Dawson's Creek*, then his buddy Pacey Witter is the anti-hero. Dawson is an idealist, struggling to be Mr. Perfect in an imperfect world; Pacey is a realist who lives according to impulses rather than rational thoughts. Dawson is in touch with his feelings and discusses them in the open (sometimes a little too often), but Pacey, who often buries his true emotions under layers of sarcasm and cool, tells his friend, "I'm not cursed with self-awareness like you are."

In any other moral universe, Pacey might seem like the average sort of smart-aleck, brazen 15-year-old kid who's suffered the ignominy of constant browbeating from an asshole of an older brother (Doug, a police deputy), and whose strained relationship with his father is complicated by the fact that Dad is the biggest authority figure in town, the police chief. But, standing next to the self-righteous Dawson, Pacey has become the show's resident "bad boy," even though many of his so-called transgressions (like losing his virginity to his English teacher, Tamara Jacobs) are merely the actions of a boy plunging headlong into manhood, embracing life to the fullest. That's why, for many female fans of the show, Pacey is the one who's All That, while Dawson is just a pretender of sorts.

"Generally speaking, they prefer Dawson," Pacey's alter-ego, actor Joshua Jackson, said of the viewers in a May 1998 *Dallas Morning News* interview. "He's more the heartthrob.

Pacey's a flawed character. Perhaps people relate to that more. You get to see the imperfections, the chinks in his armor."

Pacey's activities during the first one-and-a-half seasons of *Dawson's Creek* bear out Jackson's theory. During the first season, his torrid affair with his teacher began when he wooed her with a copy of the romantic drama *Summer of '42* from the local video-rental store (a pretty smooth move for a kid who's always had trouble with girls); it later turned into the town scandal, complete with a school board inquiry. Ms. Jacobs resigned and left the community in shame, but Pacey had to stay behind and suffer small-town ridicule.

In the second season, Pacey's poor grades and other personal problems eroded his already poor relationship with his father; at one point, Pacey even decked him with a punch in the mouth. Chastened by the crash-and-burn of his hot-for-teacher romance, Pacey waited a while before going to bed with his new girlfriend, Andie McPhee; shortly thereafter, the girl's own inner turmoil drove her mad. Some fans feared that Pacey was going soft in the second season, but Jackson told an interviewer for YM magazine, just before the show began filming its 1999–2000 season episodes: "Don't worry. We're going to make him bad again."

When he joined the *Dawson's Creek* cast at age 19, Joshua Jackson was already an accomplished actor; most notably he was a veteran of Disney's three *Mighty Ducks* films about a haphazard ice hockey team. His acting career began at age nine when he asked his mother, a casting director who worked for TV and film productions in the Vancouver area, to take him on an audition. Jackson won a role in a TV commercial promoting tourism in British Columbia; the spot aired across North America. Following this promising start, his mom took him to auditions for several productions filmed in the Vancouver area including the TV series *MacGyver* and a film

Joshua doing the WB Winter Press Tour.

called *Crooked Hearts* with Vincent D'Onofrio, Noah Wyle, and Juliette Lewis (he won both roles). He then went to Seattle and played Charlie in a stage version of *Willy Wonka and the Chocolate Factory*; an agent from the William Morris Agency was in the crowd and signed him up. Due to his busy schedule and his general dislike for formal schooling, Jackson eventually dropped out of Kitsilano High School in Vancouver and took the GED, a high school equivalency examination.

In 1992, when he was just 14, he got his first truly major break in the role of Charlie Conway, the sensitive, intro-spective child whose mother is courted by Emilio Estevez, in *The Mighty Ducks*. Jackson reprised the role in *D2: The Mighty Ducks* (1994), and in the final entry in the hockey trilogy, *D3: The Mighty Ducks* (1996), Jackson's character was moved to center stage while Emilio Estevez was relegated to the background. The critics took notice of Jackson's emergence. "With Estevez appearing in a very supporting role, the film truly rests on Jackson's shoulders," a reviewer for *Variety* wrote. "He graduates with grace from foil to front man, demonstrating a commanding, likable personality." After that film, Jackson had a small role opposite Ian McKellan and Brad Renfro in the Neo-Nazi thriller *Apt Pupil*, which was based on a Stephen King novel and directed by Bryan (*The Usual Suspects*) Singer. But then, at age 17, he came to a crossroads in his young life. "I was like, 'You know what? It's time to get a real job and put my feet back on the ground for awhile.'" So, he enrolled at the University of British Columbia. But then came the *Dawson's Creek* audition, which foiled his educational plans.

Jackson was in Los Angeles, working on a television show in which he had a small guest role, when the *Creek* audition came to his attention. "They [the producers] were desperate because all the other roles had been cast," Jackson told the *Toronto Star* in a March 1998 interview. "I got it very quickly

Joshua at the 12th annual Boston Music Awards.

and the day I finished the other thing, they put me on an all-night flight to Wilmington, North Carolina, where they had already started filming. I got off and directly went to the set and started acting." Jackson's film career has also benefited from his association with Kevin Williamson, though perhaps not the way his co-stars' careers have. In 1998, Jackson made his requisite appearance (as all Williamson cadre members must do) in a teen horror picture, a small role in *Urban Legend*; then he appeared in one of those "edgy" 1990s teen films, *Cruel Intentions*, a sort of *Dangerous Liaisons* meets *Fast Times at Ridgemont High*. Jackson's appearance in this film is noteworthy for two reasons: first, he dyed his hair blond to give his character, Blaine Tuttle, a sort of neo-teen-hipster look, and second, because Jackson's character was gay, and the role required a bedroom scene with actor Eric Mabius (of *Welcome to the Dollhouse* fame). "I looked at him and I was, like, 'This guy is ripped,'" Jackson said in the March 1999 issue of the gay men's magazine, *Out*. "I'm a skinny little beanstalk. He was probably hitting the gym, and I looked like a slug. That killed me. But then we had a couple of good laughs, shook our asses at the crew and hopped into bed."

Off-camera, Jackson is known to his fellow *Creek* cast members as the comic relief; and also a boy with a brain. "Josh is the class clown, on the show and in real life," Meredith Monroe (Andie McPhee) told YM magazine. "Josh is one of the smartest people I've ever met. He'll be talking about a poet one minute and some country's government the next. He has the most extensive information in his brain."

Incidentally, the good boy/bad boy comparison between Dawson and Pacey also holds true, to a certain extent, with the actors who play them: James Van Der Beek prefers the earnest, easily swallowed alterna-pop music found on the *Dawson's Creek* soundtrack; Joshua Jackson listens to Nirvana and hip-hop.

JOSHUA JACKSON FILMOGRAPHY

Crooked Hearts (1991, young Tom); *Mighty Ducks* (1992, Charlie); *Digger* (1993, Billy); *Andre* (1994, Mark Baker); *D2: The Mighty Ducks* (1994, Charlie); *Magic in the Water* (1995, Joshua Black); *Robin of Locksley* (1996, John Prince Jr.); *D3: The Mighty Ducks* (1996, Charlie); *On the Edge of Innocence* (1997, TV movie); *Scream 2* (1997, film student); *Apt Pupil* (1998, Joey); *Urban Legend* (1998, Damon Brooks); *Cruel Intentions* (1999, Blaine Tuttle); *Muppets From Space* (1999, cameo as himself); *Skulls* (2000, Luke McNamara).

ALMOST A WOMAN, STILL A KID
MICHELLE WILLIAMS
(JENNIFER "JEN" LINDLEY)

BIRTHDATE: September 9, 1980
BIRTHPLACE: Kalispell, Montana
EDUCATION: Home-schooled
STATS: Height: 5'4"; Eyes: Green; Hair: Blond

In the greater scheme of things it may not be the most lofty debate topic, but many *Dawson's Creek* fans are prone to discussing it: Jen versus Joey. Who's right for Dawson Leery? Who's prettier? Who's the hottie and who's the geek? Who's a bitch and who's not? Who's portrayed by a better actress?

Who knows? But one thing is certain: when Michelle Williams arrived in tiny Capeside and Dawson's eye started to wander, a nation of adolescent viewers became transfixed by the been-around-the-block girl. It's not just that Williams plays the role of femme fatale on the show, nor her sexy baby-doll looks. It's a self-assured, wise-beyond-her-years quality that Williams brings to the role. Although she is the youngest principal cast member, Williams has an impressive résumé of acting credits dating back to when she was just a single-digit kid, and her years of work on stage and in front of cameras lends a wonderful poise to her acting style. This same sense of worldliness is also evident in her personality; in published interviews, Williams does not shy away from questions about the themes running through *Dawson's Creek* — such as sex, trust, or identity — but rather, she often philosophizes about them (take that, Shannen Doherty). And she's not afraid to point out that many people out there in TV-land just don't "get" where her character is coming from.

"For a lot of people, she [Jen] is the first character that they judge," Williams said in a 1999 interview with the *Mr.*

Showbiz web site. "The show is written that way, because she's sort of 'the other woman,' taking Dawson away from Joey. So a lot of girls think that she's a bit of a bitch for that. But I just think that Jen is one of those girls who it's easy to make surface judgments about. If you take the opportunity to look past that, you'll find that she's somebody who's just as vulnerable and complex as all the rest of the characters."

Williams' role as the new girl in town, the outsider, somewhat mirrors her own life story. She was eight years old and living in Montana with her family when she saw a local stage play and asked her folks for acting lessons. A year later, the family moved to San Diego, California, and Williams began working in community theater. At 14, she appeared in her first feature film, a remake of *Lassie* (1994), and the following year she had small parts in two science-fiction movies: the low-budget *Timemasters* and the big-budget *Species*. In the latter, she played the young incarnation of Sil, a genetically engineered alien-human interbreed that grows up to resemble the beautiful Natasha Henstridge. But being a kid from another state *and* a precocious child actress who was already appearing in movies wasn't easy. She became withdrawn, and for a time she would only answer to the name "Harvey," an imaginary alter-ego. The other kids weren't always hip to that kind of stuff, so Williams' parents took her out of Santa Fe Christian High School after ninth grade and she finished her education at home, taught by her father. "It's tough. When you're new, everyone's looking at you. Adults appreciate vulnerability, but kids pounce on it. So you have to put up a good front. I tried to be stronger, better, tougher," she remembered in an interview with USA *Weekend* in 1998.

Williams passed the high school equivalency test and in 1996, at age 16, she was legally emancipated from her parents and moved to Los Angeles to pursue acting full-time (although the parting of ways was difficult, Williams reportedly has

Michelle on the set of *Lassie*.

mended her relationship with her parents and sometimes receives care packages of socks and underwear from her mom, Carla). "I came to L.A. so wide-eyed, the picture of fresh-faced innocence — and so fucking excited," she said in a 1999 interview with *Paper* magazine. "I just thought I would work! I just thought I would play cool parts." She played film and TV parts, but they weren't always cool. In 1996–97, she played Michelle Pfeiffer's daughter, Pammy, in the drama *A Thousand Acres* (1997) and landed many small parts on various teleseries (like *Baywatch*, *Home Improvement*) and TV movies (like *My Son is Innocent* and *Killing Mr. Griffin*). She also went to a lot of auditions and appeared in non-paying student and low-budget films to beef up her résumé.

Like her *Dawson's Creek* cohorts, Williams watched her star power soar as the show's popularity grew. Director Stephen Miner, who had helmed several *Dawson's Creek* episodes, cast Williams as Josh Harnett's girlfriend in *Halloween: H20* (1998), but the film really gave her nothing much to sink her teeth into. But, the following year, Williams showed great range and comic timing in the Watergate spoof *Dick* (1999), described by one critic as "*Clueless* meets *All the President's Men.*" In the movie, directed by Andrew Fleming, Williams plays Arlene, a high school student living with her single mom (Teri Garr) in the Watergate apartment complex. One night, while sneaking out to drop their entry in a "win a date with Bobby Sherman" contest into a mailbox, Arlene and her pal Betsy (Kirsten Dunst) unwittingly bump into the Watergate burglars. The girls have no idea what's going on, but President Nixon, Haldeman, Liddy, and the various Watergate culprits think the kids are on to something, so they try to win their silence by appointing the girls "official White House dog walkers" and giving them special access to the president. Arlene comically develops a crush on Tricky Dick, but when she stumbles onto one of his secret Oval Office tapes and hears him uttering four-letter words on it, her image of the president is shattered. Soon the girls become the famous "Deep Throat" source who allegedly helped reporters Woodward and Bernstein bring down the Nixon administration. Williams and Dunst are both excellent as the ditzy teens, and this film is brilliantly hilarious, but it failed miserably at the box office when released in summer 1999, owing mostly to studio marketing blunders (advertisements placed Williams and Dunst in prominent view to emphasize the teen appeal, but the subject matter was of more interest to the over-30 crowd).

Also in summer 1999, Williams made her off-Broadway debut in the play *Killer Joe*, replacing actress Fairuza Balk as Dottie, a girl proffered up by her white-trash parents as partial payment to a hit man for his services. The role required her to strip completely naked onstage, which isn't much of a shock at first, considering Williams' image as a budding sex-bomb. At the winter 1998 TV press tour, when the WB Network introduced the *Dawson's Creek* stars to the media, journalists reportedly gasped when Williams showed up "wearing stiletto heels so high she wobbled, and a dress so tight and oh, so Marilyn Monroe," wrote a reporter for *UltimateTV*) and all the magazine photo layouts she did in 1998 and 1999 featured her in androgynous poses or casting alluring looks into the lens. Therefore, it *is* something of a surprise to learn that Williams has what she calls "huge body issues," and she doesn't read beauty magazines because they make her depressed. But this apparent conflict — uncomfortable with her physical appearance yet willing to bare it all for her art — is part of the actress's complex personality.

While not filming the show in Wilmington, Williams keeps an apartment in Sherman Oaks, California, but she hardly ever gets to stay there. She is romantically unattached, and as she told *Paper*, she prefers men of the "renegade" variety, those who

Kirsten Dunst and Michelle Williams, friends on screen and off.

fall somewhere between the Dawson and Pacey varieties. And, as one critic observed: "Any fellow who falls for her had better be prepared to appreciate her brain, as she has a definite philosophical bent, and is an avid reader [of] such highbrow authors as Hermann Hesse, Fyodor Dostoyevsky, and Kurt Vonnegut, Jr."

MICHELLE WILLIAMS FILMOGRAPHY

Lassie (1994, April); *Species* (1995, young Sil); *Timemasters* (1995, Annie); *My Son Is Innocent* (1996 TV movie); *Killing Mr. Griffin* (1997 TV movie, Susan); *Kangaroo Palace* (1997 TV mini-series, Mrs. Lafont); *A Thousand Acres* (1997, Pammy); *Halloween: H20* (1998, Molly); *If These Walls Could Talk 2* (1999 TV movie); *Dick* (1999, Arlene Lorenzo); *But I'm a Cheerleader* (1999, Kimberly).

PASS THE VALIUM
MEREDITH MONROE
(ANDIE MCPHEE)

BIRTHDATE: December 30, 1976

BIRTHPLACE: Houston, Texas

EDUCATION: Hinsdale Central High School (Hinsdale, Illinois)

STATS: Height: 5′6 ½″; Eyes: Brown; Hair: Blond

There's plenty of angst and identity crises to go around in *Dawson's Creek*, but no character is as seriously unhinged as Andie. When she and her then-closeted brother Jack moved to the town of Capeside to escape their terrible past, she should have left her baggage at home. In the course of one abbreviated television season, Andie's itinerary took her across the histrionic spectrum: she charmed that badass Pacey and helped turn him into a nice guy; she came to the aid of her crazy mom; she defended her neo-homosexual brother from the town's homophobes; she did the wild thang with Pacey; she swallowed lots of anti-depressants; she went off her medication; and then (most interestingly) she went insane, unraveled by the death of her friend Abby. She started seeing the ghost of her dead older brother, Tim, and scissored off most of her blond locks and dyed the rest of 'em brown. In short, this chick is wacked.

"What's going to happen to me?" Andie asked, crying in Pacey's arms, in the last episode of *Dawson's* second season, before leaving Capeside in search of mental stability. As we wait to see what happens when Andie's emotional rollercoaster returns for another ride in Season Three, it is undeniable that the character helped lend another level of drama to the otherwise sex-focused lives of the *Creek* gang, due largely to the performance of Meredith Monroe, an ebullient young product model–turned–actress with some of the most impressive dramatic skills among the cast. What started out as a bubbly, full-of-life teen descended into the depths of madness and ended up a damaged soul, and Monroe captured both extremes of her character equally well.

An only child whose parents divorced when she was just two years old, Monroe was born in Houston and raised in Hinsdale, Illinois (a well-to-do Chicago suburb) by her mother, who worked for Lucent Technologies; she also spent summers with her father, a computer-company manager, in Florida and Texas. After graduating from high school, Monroe moved to New York to begin modeling; by 1995, she was appearing steadily in TV commercials and magazine ads for such items as L'Oréal hair-care products, Huffy bicycles, Mattel toys, Ford cars — heck, she was even in one of those stupid-but-fun Mentos "the freshmaker" commercials, and she's had her picture on the box of a hair-crimping iron. Even with her work on *Dawson's Creek*, Monroe's modeling career continues — in 1999, she appeared in a 7-Up soft drink commercial.

Monroe made the transition to acting in 1996, when she was cast as Tracy Dalken in three episodes toward the end of the 1996–97 season on the ABC series *Dangerous Minds*. Monroe was told she would return the following season in a recurring role, but then the show was canceled. No matter — her work on *Dangerous Minds* attracted enough attention to get her a series of television appearances on shows like *Players*, the soap opera *Sunset Beach* (as a pregnant teen), *Promised Land*, and *Night Man*.

Monroe credits her love of *Buffy the Vampire Slayer* with preparing her for the part of Andie: when the WB Network moved *Buffy* to Tuesday nights to segue into this new program called *Dawson's Creek* in spring 1998, Monroe kept glued to the tube and became a regular viewer; when the audition came up soon thereafter, in June 1998, she was well attuned to the show's emotionally heightened vibe. "It was great when I found out I had the audition because I already knew all the characters and everything that had been going on in the storyline," Monroe said in an interview posted on the WB Television Network Web site. Monroe's boyfriend, identified only as "Steve," a massage therapist, accompanied her to the audition, as he usually does; when it was over, she thought she had blown it. But, the following Tuesday, the good news came.

"Andie was an especially hard role to cast," *Dawson's Creek* executive producer Paul Stupin told *Soap Opera Digest* in 1999. "Because we were looking for a real sense of quirkiness and intelligence and dynamism, coupled with what we hoped would be a wonderful look. Many an actress came, but none that we really felt was the perfect match of the character with the person. Then Meredith came in, and after she left the room, we all thought, 'there's Andie.'"

Dawson's Creek creator Kevin Williamson was equally impressed: "I met with her to get to know her after I saw her [audition] tape," Williamson told the *Official Site of Meredith Monroe* in February 1999. "It's inspiring when we're developing the character to see if [the portrayer] sparks something in us to take the character in a fresher direction. I walked away from that lunch completely inspired in terms of where to take the character of Andie."

More recently, Monroe played Laura Ingalls Wilder, upon whose life story the *Little House on the Prairie* teleseries was based, in the 1999 TV movie *Beyond the Prairie: The True Story of Laura Ingalls Wilder*. She also appeared in a feature film, *Mary Jane's Last Dance*, to be released in 2000.

But what her fans invariably want to know is this: How close is that crazy-ass Andie to the real Meredith Monroe? "She is so much like me," she told *Soap Opera Digest*. "I can be very anal and uptight about things like school or bills . . . I'm always

Meredith Monroe at the 1999 TV Guide Awards.

prepared; I'm always on time. I'm always the one thinking of the consequences of any action. But, on the other hand, sometimes I'm just like the goofiest, most off-the-wall person and I'll say the weirdest thing. People are like, 'where are you from?'"

MEREDITH MONROE FILMOGRAPHY

Fallen Arches (1998, Karissa); *Beyond the Prairie: The True Story of Laura Ingalls Wilder* (1999 TV movie, Laura Ingalls).

BOYS WILL BE BOYS
KERR SMITH
(JACK MCPHEE)

BIRTHDATE: March 9, 1972
BIRTHPLACE: Exton, Pennsylvania
EDUCATION: Bachelor's degree in finance and accounting,
University of Vermont, 1994

What's more difficult for an actor: posing buck naked in front of one of the most desirable teen starlets (and, by extension, in front of a TV crew and the TV teen nation) or playing a gay guy on a TV show with a huge female following?

Given Kevin Williamson's penchant for blurring the line between reality and fiction, actor Kerr Smith may end up receiving fewer fan letters from girls than his male co-stars, since that fateful episode in February 1999 when Jack McPhee proclaimed his homosexuality to the prime-time world. But Smith doesn't seem to mind. Like Van Der Beek, Jackson, Holmes, and Williams, the young actor has been quickly propelled to the forefront of American pop culture by the success of *Dawson's Creek* and, even though he is very much a supporting player, Jack has garnered more headlines than that of any other *Creek* character.

As an actor, Smith says he accepted Jack's coming-out as a challenge (it must have been quite a challenge to convince audiences that Jack is gay, because he showed absolutely no such leanings beforehand). And as a 20-something American citizen, he accepted it as a positive role-model for young people and their attitudes toward gays. "On one hand I felt really good about it, but on the other hand I felt kind of scared," Smith told *Entertainment Weekly Online* in March 1999, a few weeks after Jack's revelation. "A friend told me he read on the Internet about a kid who told his parents he was gay right after watching the show. I wasn't quite ready for that. It's a lot of responsibility, and, not knowing we were going this way when I was cast [Smith was informed of Williamson's decision to make Jack gay in October 1998, after the season was already in full swing], I didn't ask for this responsibility. But I've accepted it and we're going ahead. I would like to think we're helping people."

At first, Jack McPhee seemed like a typical, angst-ridden character among the *Dawson's Creek* entourage, but things began getting difficult for him in the weeks of early 1999. A sadistic English teacher (as always, in Kevin Williamson's universe, teachers aren't nice) forced Jack to stand up in class and read a poem that sounded an awful lot as if it were written by a gay guy; soon thereafter, nasty rumors about Jack were swirling around the Capeside community, and a homophobic slur was scrawled on his school locker. Jack tried to reassure Joey, his then-girlfriend, that he was straight as an arrow but finally he came clean about it and told her yes, he's gay; Joey did the only thing a crushed girl can do: she ran weeping back into the arms of Dawson, her ex. Jack also had to break the news to his cold, uncaring father. Fans of the show, however, were more sympathetic to Jack's plight. "It was about a teenager struggling with his sexuality, rather than all of a sudden having a gay character in *Dawson's Creek*," Smith told *Soap Opera Digest*. "You've got to tell it like it really happens, and I think we've accomplished that. The response was unbelievable."

Kerr Smith is the oldest member of the *Dawson's Creek* cast; he was 25 when the show premiered. Considering his back-ground as a soap opera actor, it's easy to assume that "Kerr" is a soapy pseudonym, but it's not: Smith got his funny first name from his grandmother. He grew up in the suburban

Philadelphia area and, by all media accounts, he was a normal kid, a competitive athlete, and Associated Student Body President of his high school. Smith first flirted with acting in his sophomore year of high school when he enrolled in a drama class, and soon he was in a school production of *The King and I.* But after high school he decided to follow in his father's footsteps and he went to the University of Vermont to study finance and accounting. After completing his degree, he moved back to Pennsylvania and worked at his father's marketing firm. But his thespian yearnings still tugged at him. He began making trips to New York for open auditions; in the process he got himself an agent. But commuting back-and-forth between Philly and New York took a lot out of him, so he soon sold his Ford Bronco and used the money to move to New York and pursue his dreams full time. There was an audition for the long-running soap opera *As The World Turns,* and although he didn't get the part that he read for, Smith was cast as Ryder Hughes. His 1996–97 stint on the soap earned Smith the Best New Actor award from *Soap Opera Magazine.*

Not content to merely fill the mid-day lives of housewives and old ladies with entertainment, Smith set out for bigger acting conquests. In early 1998 he drove to Los Angeles (along with his girlfriend, Ali Hillis, who has appeared in small roles on *Felicity* and other programs) and auditioned for the TV series *Party of Five.* He didn't get that part, but a top casting director at the WB Network took notice of Smith and, several months later, when *Dawson's Creek* was being cast, Smith got that Phone Call That Changed His Life. Since then, he's also made a guest appearance on the classic T-&-A series *Baywatch* and appeared in a feature film called *Flight 180* for New Line Cinema that will be released in 2000; two other independent films that he appeared in during his struggling New York days, titled *Kiss & Tell* (the story of four couples on a televised blind

Kerr Smith

date) and *Hit and Runaway* (in which he plays a gay man), may also be released in the future, perhaps as straight-to-video fare.

So, what's more difficult, posing in the buff or being the gay guy? In one of *Dawson's Creek*'s classic second-season moments, Jack spilled a drink on Joey's drawing pad, ruining a sketch of a nude model she'd done in her art class. In a tribute to the scene in *Titanic* wherein Kate Winslet reclines nude on a couch for Leonardo DiCaprio's pencil strokes, Jack agrees to strip down and pose so Joey can redo her school assignment. Smith says that Jack's coming-out was tougher. "I don't really have a problem with being naked," he told *Soap Opera Digest*. "Although for 12 hours in front of 40 people who are not naked, it's not exactly fun."

KERR SMITH FILMOGRAPHY

Twelve Monkeys (1995, extra); *Kiss & Tell* (1999, Kelly); *Hit and Runaway* (1999, Joey); *Flight 180* (2000, Carter).

Baldwin, Kristen. "The Monroe doctrine." *Entertainment Weekly*. May 21, 1999.

Bawden, Jim. "*Dawson's Creek's* Joshua Jackson can't believe it came so fast." *Toronto Star*. March 12, 1998.

Bonin, Liane. "Jack's flash." *Entertainment Weekly Online*. Online. March 17, 1999.

"Celebrities; Star Bio: Katie Holmes" *Mr. Showbiz*. Online.

"Celebrities; Star Bio: James Van Der Beek." *Mr. Showbiz*. Online.

"Celebrities; Star Bio: Michelle Williams." abc *News Internet Ventures*. Online.

Cogshell, Tim. "The *Mr. Showbiz* interview: Michelle Williams." *Mr. Showbiz*. Online. 1999.

Dunn, Jancee. "Katie Holmes, a girl on the verge." *Rolling Stone*. September 17, 1998.

Epstein, Jeffrey. "Andie land." *Soap Opera Digest*. February 2, 1999.

—. "Captain Kerr-ageous." *Soap Opera Digest*. April 19, 1999.

Goldsmith, Sarah. "Backstage pass: Dawson's peak." *Seventeen*. February 1999.

Hobson, Louis B. "Teaching Katie Holmes; *Dawson's Creek* star's career blossoming." *Calgary Sun*. August 15, 1999.

Huff, Richard. "Dawson's damsel in demand." *New York Daily News*. May 16, 1999.

Lipton, Michael A. and Paula Yoo. "*Creek* god." *People*. April 1998.

McCarthy, Mandy. "Kerr Smith." *UltimateTV News*. Online. November 1, 1998

McIntyre, Grant. "Profile: Joshua then and now." *Broadcast Week*. April 11–17, 1998.

Meeson, Andrew. "Teen actor shows his smarts." *Globe and Mail*. April 11, 1998.

Mendoza, N.F. "Michelle Williams." *UltimateTV*. Online. July 22, 1998.

"Modest Van Der Beek is a 'Varsity' team player." *USA Today*. January 28, 1999.

Sarko, Anita. "Naked angel." *Paper*. July 1999.

Smith, Chris and Holly Sorensen. "The kids of *Dawson's Creek*" *US*. May 1998.

Vitrano, Alyssa. "Meredith rocks the creek." *YM* Magazine. June 1999.

Wolf, Jeanne. "Holmes Sweet Holmes." *E! Online*. Online. 1999

The following Internet web sites were also consulted:

Internet Movie Database (www.imdb.com)
Unofficial Kerr Smith Website (advicom.net/~e-media/kv/kerr.htm)
The Official Site of Meredith Monroe (www.meredithmonroe.com)

PORTRAIT OF THE ARTIST
AS A YOUNG MAN

To understand the phenomenon that is *Dawson's Creek*, you must first understand the phenomenon and youth mogul who is Kevin Williamson. In just three years, Williamson went from being a struggling scribe living in a low-rent L.A. apartment and attending screenwriting courses at UCLA's extension school to the most high-profile writer in Hollywood (stealing that title away from its previous holder, Quentin Tarantino). He now boasts a $20-million development deal from Miramax Films, residences on both coasts (an apartment in Greenwich Village and an antique-filled house in the stately Hancock Park section of L.A.), and a wide-ranging influence on the entertainment produced for the all-important teenage-to-early-twenties demographic group. In short, between 1996 and 1998, Williamson re-invented the stale teen horror movie genre when his first produced screenplay, the horror film *Scream*, blew Hollywood away by grossing $106 million in the U.S. and more than $165 million internationally (it cost just $12 million to make, and is now the highest-grossing horror movie of all time). A series of self-referential sequels and similar movies full of Williamsonesque pop-culture references followed. Then, he revitalized the ever-popular teen TV soap opera with *Dawson's Creek*, and he helped make bona fide movie stars out of the attractive young actresses populating his work like Jennifer Love Hewitt, Sarah Michelle Gellar, and

Creek stars Michelle Williams and Katie Holmes. In just two years, Williamson has accrued more credits on his résumé than many writers do in their entire careers, and he has been lauded by the media as the voice of a generation (not his own, but that of kids some 10 to 15 years younger than him). Today, if you're a player in Hollywood, you want to work with this man, because almost everything he touches turns to gold. But if you're an aspiring screenwriter toiling away on an old Smith-Corona, you hate his guts, because he makes it look so easy.

In published interviews, Williamson is often described as shy and self-effacing, a man who continues to embrace and revisit the ideals of his formative years well into his thirties, and perhaps a bit emotionally immature (during the publicity blitz for *Teaching Mrs. Tingle* in summer 1999, Williamson mentioned to more than one interviewer that he was currently feuding with his boyfriend). It has been written more than once that the key to Williamson's success as a writer is his ability to address teen issues in frank terms that his audience can relate to, even if the dialogue spouted by his characters is more articulate than the "ums," "know what I'm sayin's," and assorted profane grunts sputtering out of the average teen's mouth. He has earned credibility with his audience because of his ability to speak to teenagers on their level without being perceived as an adult who's pandering to them in order to cash in. Sarah Michelle Gellar, who co-starred in *I Know What You Did Last Summer* and *Scream 2*, once told the *Boston Globe* that Williamson "talks to our generation. These kids in Kevin's movies are smart. We, the audience, don't look down on them because Kevin doesn't look down on us. Before, it was the bimbo running through the woods, or back up the stairs of a dark house with no one else in the house and with the phone lines down. Now, maybe you'll still be killed, but you fight like hell. You may die, but you're fighting up until the end.

You're not the helpless heroine anymore."

But, on the flipside, Williamson is also a pragmatist — his keen awareness of the marketplace is another major reason for his success, particularly in the early going. In 1997, Williamson told the *New York Times* that, before he wrote *Scream*, "I looked around and asked myself: What's missing from the marketplace? The answer was a scary movie populated with young kids, so the young audience will see it. . . . It was a calculated business move. I was hoping it would pay off." It *did* pay off and, despite all the praise heaped upon him in recent years, Williamson keeps a clear perspective on his work, freely admitting that his material is a mass-market product, not art. "I'm not a real writer; I'm a screenwriter," he told *Time Out New York* magazine in 1999. "[Screenwriting is] not a real art form. It's movies. We're not curing cancer here . . . I just write the way I talk — that's why it's so grammatically incorrect."

Williamson was born March 14, 1965, in New Bern, North Carolina, and raised in the tiny fishing village of Oriental, North Carolina (so small it's not even on most maps), a place that actually had a little spot called Dawson's Creek, where the teens would go to skinny-dip and make out (the sort of place he would later incorporate into the fictional backdrop of Capeside, Massachusetts). His father, Wade, was a fisherman who ran a 105-foot-long trawler with a crew of five; during his father's long absences at sea, Williamson's mother, Faye, would entertain little Kevin and his older brother, John, with stories. This, Williamson says, is how his dreams of becoming a writer — moreover, a storyteller — were formed. "My dad has this dry sense of humor, but he never wanted me or my brother to become fishermen," Wiliamson told the *San Francisco Chronicle* in 1997. "He wanted us to go to college." His mother, Williamson added, is "the storyteller who gave me that gift, and the inspiration. . . .

She could take any circumstance and make a great tale out of it." Williamson has likened the environment of his young life to that of *The Waltons*, one of his favorite TV series. "We didn't have a lot of money, but we weren't white trash," he told *The Advocate* in 1999. "I had wonderful parents, and they always provided. I always got what I wanted." Years later, when Williamson began recycling the places, situations, and people from his childhood into dramatic material, even his parents were not exempt: the stalking fisherman-killer from *I Know What You Did Last Summer* was partly inspired by his father's occupation (fishing, not killing) and in Williamson's 1999 directorial debut film, *Teaching Mrs. Tingle*, Leslie Ann Warren's character Faye was named after Williamson's mom. His southern upbringing "led me to wanting to be a storyteller," Williamson said, "because I always felt I was born in the wrong place, sleeping by the television every night and longing to be in New York. And so I went there in my imagination."

Kevin gets his face painted before a high school production, in which he played Jake the Snake.

During the 1970s, Williamson and his family lived for a time in rural Aransas Pass, Texas, and it was there that he became a young movie buff. "My mom would drop me off at Rialto, which was the only theater in town," he told the *Los Angeles Times* in 1999 (incidentally, the *Stab* sequence in *Scream 2* was filmed at the same-named Rialto Theater in South Pasadena, California). "I'd get there in time for the

Jake the Snake

first movie and stay until my mom picked me up at 9 p.m. I saw *Jaws* there, *Airport 1975*, *Benji*, and *Star Wars*. The kids stormed the theater for *Jaws*. It was a mob scene." In those pre-VCR days, Williamson once spent an entire day watching six consecutive showings of *Halloween*. Those days at the local bijou became a ritual and were intertwined with other, seemingly more important landmarks in Williamson's young life — for instance, he remembers his mother explaining the facts of life to him on one of those Sundays in the car on the way to see the Robert Redford spy thriller *Three Days of the Condor*; this sort of interplay between real-life drama and pop-culture entertainment no doubt accounts for the emotionally charged, media-savvy lives that many of Williamson's characters live. Those Sundays at the movies fueled dreams of one day becoming a filmmaker (Williamson has credited *Jaws* with first inspiring him to make movies). At age 12, Williamson convinced the local librarian to subscribe to the showbiz trade paper *Variety* so he could read about Hollywood goings-on, and he studied the craft of pop

storytelling through reading his parents' novels by Louis L'Amour, Clive Cussler, and Arthur Hailey; he also read Syd Field's famous screenwriting books (which are like bibles to any serious film scribe). By age 13, he was making Super 8mm movies in his backyard, editing them on one of those old two-reel film editors purchased from a Sears Roebuck catalog.

Despite the multiple film and television projects he juggles today, writing wasn't easy for Williamson at first. In high school, an English teacher continually derided his lousy grammar, bad sentence structure, and poor spelling, and repeatedly told him that he would never make it, that he was a no-account, grammatically challenged hick. The teacher's words so rattled young Kevin that he perceived himself a failure; in fact, Williamson continued to be so obsessed with his shortcomings as a writer that, many years later, when he wrote his first screenplay, it was an attempt to exorcise some of those demons. The screenplay, *Killing Mrs. Tingle*, was inspired by that teacher who gave him his first terrible reviews — in the story, Williamson takes figurative revenge on his tormentor through the actions of the characters, high school students who confront their teacher because of the poor grades she's given them. "I really had that teacher," Williamson told the *Toronto Sun* in 1998, "and she tried to kill me. To this day, I do not know why she chose to hate me so much." He related his harrowing experiences with the teacher this way: "It was English and I was reading my short story about date rape to the class. Halfway through she stopped me, gave me an 'F' and told me I had no business writing anything, and that my voice should not be heard. I didn't write again for 10 years."

Williamson was president of his high school drama club, before attending East Carolina University on an acting scholarship. He studied theater and film, and also took writing courses, wherein the instructors reportedly again told him that his talents probably lie elsewhere. After graduating from college, Williamson went to New York with aspirations of becoming an actor, appeared in several stage productions, and landed a minor role as a character named "Dougie" on the NBC soap opera *Another World* in 1990. Then, Williamson went to Los Angeles, where he continued acting (he once played William Kennedy Smith opposite Jim Carrey in a skit on Fox's *In Living Color*) and was an assistant to a music video-director (Williamson worked on LL Cool J's "Mama Said Knock You Out" video, among others). But soon he was fired from the music-video job and he found himself drifting. He worked as a waiter in a restaurant, as a word processor for a temporary employment agency, and he walked dogs for the well-to-do. Although he wasn't exactly starving, it was a time of struggle for the young artist, who was still trying to find his creative niche. "There's so much mental anguish over not knowing what you're going to do next, not having a direction. It's a very scary place not to know where you're going with your life and feeling that you truly have no reason to wake up in the morning," he later told the Minneapolis *Star Tribune*. Williamson found his much-needed direction when a friend loaned him money to take screenwriting classes at UCLA's night school. But Williamson says his mother knew all along that he would one day be a scribe. "I called her and said I was gonna try out this writing thing. And she said, 'So you finally got the hint from when I gave you the typewriter when you were 10,'" he told the *Chicago Tribune* in 1997. The typewriter was a Christmas present. "She had it gift-wrapped, and left it in the back seat of the car," but a holiday Grinch broke into the car and stole it; his dad had to borrow money to replace the typewriter. "They were your basic Southern parents, they'd sacrifice anything for the kids." A few years after he enrolled at UCLA, that old typewriter would start to pay off and he'd

Kevin's senior class photo.

repay his parents for their support by buying them a new house in their hometown of New Bern. Subsequently, in 1994, he finished the afore-mentioned *Killing Mrs. Tingle* screenplay, landed an agent who soon sold the script, and proceeded to live off his earnings for the next year. "I was desperate, broke and down on my luck in L.A., and I took this [screenwriting] class as a kind of exploration," he told the *San Francisco Chronicle*. "It made me settle into story-telling. I've been writing ever since. In fact, it just gushes out."

When he sold *Killing Mrs. Tingle*, Williamson surpassed the first, most insurmountable hurdle that any young screenwriter faces: getting your first script sold. And, like thousands of other writers before him, he stood a great chance (in all probability, the great likelihood) that this might be his only sale — that *Killing Mrs. Tingle* would languish in the file drawer of some production executive, and never be made (in fact, the script languished in limbo for several years, until Williamson gained enough clout to direct it himself). But inspiration came again and, as was the case with *Killing Mrs. Tingle*, it would come from a real-life incident. One night in 1995, while Williamson was house-sitting for a friend, he went to bed uneasily after watching a news program about the real-life campus serial murders in Gainesville, Florida. Soon he was awakened in the wee hours by noises in the dark. He grabbed a butcher knife and went to investigate, and when the coast was clear he telephoned a friend for moral support. Instead, the friend taunted him, whispering "kill, kill, kill" (from *Friday the 13th*) into the receiver. Their conversation eventually turned into a debate over whether the *Halloween* movies or the *Nightmare On Elm Street* series is scarier. Such heady inspiration couldn't have come at a better time, for the money Williamson earned from selling *Killing Mrs. Tingle* was fast running out. "So for three days I wrote nonstop in this friend of mine's place in [Palm Springs, California], with no phone or television, just some scary soundtrack music I brought with me," Williamson once told the *Boston Globe*. "I literally wrote the *Scream* screenplay in three days, although I had outlined it over the course of a week a couple of months before."

Williamson says that the real-life Mrs. Tingle, his old

nemesis, did not live long enough to see him prove her wrong. "I kind of look upon her fondly now that everything seems to have turned out OK," he told the Minneapolis *Star Tribune* in 1997. Alas, Mrs. Tingle never had to eat crow — she didn't witness Williamson's extraordinary, meteoric rise to the forefront of screenwriting; she didn't see him become a celebrity (an unusual distinction for a screenwriter, except those few who attain Tarantino-caliber recognition), meeting reporters for interviews at the Polo Lounge in Beverly Hills and appearing on shows like *Politically Incorrect*; she didn't see the fuss that ensued when Sony Pictures wanted to boast in its advertising for *I Know What You Did Last Summer* that the film was "from the creator of *Scream*," and Miramax Films objected, trying to keep Williamson all for itself; she didn't hear Miramax president Harvey Weinstein describe her former student as a "genius"; Mrs. Tingle didn't have to read in *Variety* that Williamson was now turning down lucrative projects that other screenwriters would kill for — like *The Exorcist Part IV*, and live-action versions of *Scooby Doo* and *Speed Racer*. By 1998, Williamson was a full-fledged phenomenon and he could afford to pick and choose films that fit the identity he was trying to establish for himself. "One of the things I've tried to do as a writer is to develop a distinct voice," he told the *Star Tribune*. "It may not be good, but at least it's different and it'll stand out a little more. If it's not successful and people don't like it, at least it was mine."

SCREAM KING:
THE FILMS OF KEVIN WILLIAMSON

In 1999, the *Los Angeles Times* asked Kevin Williamson what his favorite movie was. "*Jaws*," he answered without hesitation. "I'd love to see it again for the first time. It was the movie that made me want to be in the movie business." At other times, Williamson has expressed his love of John Carpenter's original *Halloween*, and for the films of director John Hughes, the king of 1980s teen cinema. Elements of all these influences are evident throughout Williamson's body of work — the jolting scares of *Jaws*, the mysterious masked murderer à la *Halloween*'s Michael Myers, and updated versions of the savvy, self-aware teens and Reagan-era pop-culture references that were so much a part of Hughes' films like *Ferris Bueller's Day Off* and *The Breakfast Club*.

    Scream is Williamson's first and most important film, for it immediately established him as a writer with a unique voice and an ability to deconstruct the horror genre and put it back together, all in the course of a single screenplay. And of all the films that have influenced Williamson's work, *Halloween* had the biggest impact on his approach to *Scream* — in fact, when he first set about writing a horror screenplay, he envisioned writing a modern version of the same story but ultimately realized that today's audiences are too irony-stricken to fall for the same old horror-movie riffs. Williamson's solution? Instead of letting the audience wait for all the old scary clichés, he wrote a movie in which the characters openly discuss those clichés (like the doomed, large-breasted heroines who always run right into the killer's trap), all the while being sucked into their own web of murder, mayhem, and terror. Yes, Williamson employs most of the usual tricks, but you can't criticize him for it because his deconstructionist, media-savvy characters beat you to the punch. As Williamson explained in a 1997 *Boston Globe* interview, "The average 15-year-old girl who went to see the first *Halloween* movie back in 1978 is by no means coming from the same place that the average 15-year-old girl is who saw *Scream*. . . . Not only are teenagers a lot more self-aware but now there's cable and VCRs, and kids know these kinds of movies backwards and forwards."

In *Halloween*, John Carpenter took the day that Western cultures have designated for purging fears of evil spirits, monsters, and other bugaboos and turned it inside-out, with all those imaginary fears becoming realities in the form of a killer known as "the shape," who inexplicably wears a rubber William Shatner mask. In *Scream*, Williamson did virtually the same thing, turning the fictional world of horror films into reality for his characters. Like Dawson Leery, who would follow in their footsteps a year and a half later, the characters in *Scream* are steeped in movie trivia. Knowing that many modern American high school kids grew up watching horror pictures like the *Halloween*, *Friday the 13th*, and *Nightmare on Elm Street* series, Williamson gave his characters a vast knowledge of slasher-movie rules and regulations. While the teens in *Scream* are discussing the old films wherein knife-wielding slashers chase and kill unwary, sexy teens, they themselves are being chased by their own mad killer. In this way, the film carries on a conversation with the audience — the crowd finds itself reliving past horror film favorites (indeed, the film begins with the killer calling his victim on the telephone and asking, "what's your favorite scary movie?") and trying to catch all the genre references that whiz by. And there are lots of them: A kid calls another kid "Leatherface" (a reference to *The Texas Chainsaw Massacre*); Linda Blair (the possessed child from *The Exorcist*) has a cameo; and there are direct and indirect references to *Psycho*, *Carrie*, *The Howling*, *The Silence of the Lambs*, *The Evil Dead*, *Hellraiser*, *Terror Train*, *Prom Night*, *I Spit on Your Grave*, *Candyman*, and many other films. Thus, the self-referentiality of the characters, and of the film itself, and constant use of pop references and in-jokes (often dubbed "postmodern" by critics who enjoy overusing that word) is a key element to the Williamson formula, and the primary reason why *Scream* received favorable reviews from Roger Ebert and many other well-regarded film pundits. At the same time, Williamson and director Wes Craven balance the knife-edge between terror and parody, and charge the film with real scares — which is undoubtedly why the film scored such a major hit with teen audiences.

The plot, while by no means revolutionary, also stretches the rules of the usual teen cut-'em-up movie, making it more difficult to guess where the next clue leads — for instance, Williamson uses two killers to derail the genre's tradition of physically impossible deeds. In a riff reminiscent of Hitchcock's *Psycho*, a prominent actress (Drew Barrymore) is introduced during the first reel and soon killed off. The main character, Sidney (Neve Campbell), a high school student, is left alone for the weekend; her father has gone out of town on the one-year anniversary of his wife/her mother's murder. Soon, rumors are circulating at school about cult murders in which the killer wears a Halloween costume called Father Death, with an eerie mask reminiscent of Munch's "The Scream" painting. Pretty soon, everyone in the town of Woodsboro, California is a suspect, including the girl's boyfriend and her father. The plot, essentially, is about the murders, but the plot-within-the-plot is really about the kids who realize they are part of an unfolding slasher-movie-style mystery. When Sidney rejects her boyfriend's sexual advances, another character notes that virgins (like *Halloween's* Laurie Strode) are never murdered in horror films; meanwhile, the characters discuss which actors would play their roles in the film version of the events unfolding. "I see myself as a sort of young Meg Ryan, but with my luck, I'll probably get Tori Spelling," one character laments.

"*Halloween* dealt with simple, almost primal fears of being home alone with a child and someone looking from outside and coming and getting you," Williamson said in an interview with the London *Daily Telegraph*. "But now the audience have become so culture-driven and multimedia-savvy that I wanted to have fun with that. *Halloween* is a classic urban legend: you're watching a kid and a killer comes and gets you. Whereas *Scream* is the nineties version of that urban legend: the story of the movie about the baby-sitter . . . it's very self-aware. We give everyone the rules, and then break them. So much has happened in our movie world that we can't shock the audience in the old ways. Horror movies have to exist now in the horror movie."

One area where *Scream* sticks to the usual stabber flick formula is the gore — there is lots of blood in the film, although much of the violence is diminished by the satirical tone and the irony with which death and slicing-and-dicing are presented. Surprisingly, Williamson says he is squeamish. "When I first saw *Scream*," he told the *San Francisco Chronicle* in 1997, "I complained to [director] Wes [Craven], 'This thing's so bloody and violent.' He said, 'Kevin, get a grip, you wrote it.'" Certainly much of the film's success must be attributed to Craven, who previously had established himself as one of the greatest teen-horror film directors in history with his *Nightmare on Elm Street* series and other pictures like *The Last House on the Left* and *The Hills Have Eyes*.

In *Scream*, a doomed character pleads with the killer, "Oh no, Mr. Scary Ghost Face, don't kill me, I want to be in the sequel." Williamson says that when he first submitted his treatment for *Scream*, it was the first film in a projected trilogy — a bold move for an unknown screenwriter. As it turned out, Williamson's horror trilogy would indeed become a reality, but in the meantime, the writer would begin honing his craft on *I Know What You Did Last Summer*. This, Williamson's next film, was released just before Halloween 1997 and, while it was also phenomenally successful (it cost a skimpy $16 million and made about $70 million domestically), it was almost unanimously raked over by the critics, who found little new material, aside from the slick production values and the likable young cast (featuring TV babes Jennifer Love Hewitt of *Party of Five* and Sarah Michelle Gellar of *Buffy the Vampire Slayer*). Whereas Williamson broke new ground with *Scream*'s self-referential theme of horror film fandom gone awry, *I Know What You Did* was a mostly typical kids-get-killed affair. The reason? Perhaps it was the fact that, while *Scream* was Williamson's own personal inspiration, he wrote the script for *I Know What You Did* as a hired gun.

I Know What You Did was helmed by first-time director Jim Gillespie, a Scottish-born filmmaker who had previously directed television programs in the United Kingdom with titles like *Cardiac Arrest* and *The Ghostbusters of East Finchley*. Gillespie moved to Hollywood in the early 1990s with aspirations of directing feature films; eventually he was offered a picture called *Big Bugs*, which he described as "*Jurassic Park* with insects," but he ended up walking off the project when the studio began balking at the cost of special effects. Eventually he was offered another chance with *I Know What You Did Last Summer*, the story of four former high school students from North Carolina who face the consequences of keeping quiet about their involvement in a hit-and-run accident. The story was based on a book of the same title written in the 1960s by Lois Duncan, an author of several dozen teen novels and books (Duncan, whose daughter was murdered in 1989, is also author of *Who Murdered My Daughter?* and has dedicated herself in recent years to solving her daughter's murder). *I Know What You Did Last Summer* (the book), which has been taught in middle and junior high school English classes for years, is about resisting peer pressure and doing the right thing. In interviews published at the time the movie version was released, Duncan was quoted saying she was aghast at the movie, due to all the changes made to her story and the amount of violence and blood. In the book version, there is just one death — a child on a bicycle is hit by a car, and the death is revealed in a flashback; the four teens in the car flee the scene without stopping. But in the movie, the teens, while driving home in a somewhat inebriated state from a Fourth of July celebration (actually, they've just been sitting around drinking and telling spooky stories), hit an adult, a solitary pedestrian on a country road. After an endless argument over whether the cops should be called or not, the kids decide to cover up the crime to save their own asses. Believed dead, the man's body is dumped in a lake. But he's not really dead, just very stunned. The guilty kids maintain a conspiracy of silence to protect themselves, but a year later threatening notes begin arriving, warning, "I know what you did last summer," and then the killing starts. Two of the teens are decapitated with boat hooks; another character (who does not appear in the book) is boiled alive. There's a scene where the heroine opens her car trunk to find a dead body with crabs crawling out of its mouth. The killer is a not-quite-dead and very angry longshoreman who wields a deadly fish hook and slinks around town in a rain slicker. The Gorton's fisherman he ain't.

Shot in Southport, North Carolina, *I Know What You Did* contains some of the southern settings and fishing-village aesthetics that would later become such a big part of *Dawson's Creek*. In an interview just before the film was released, Williamson told CNN *Showbiz Today*, "*Scream* was sort of my childhood love of horror films, sort of — you know, where I got to pay tribute and homage to them. *I Know What You Did*

Last Summer was . . . I love writing about teenagers, I love writing about kids, you know, and it sort of takes me back to that time. . . . I got to bring my whole childhood to life, in the sense that I got to create it around my home town. Growing up on the water, my dad was a fisherman, and a fish hook was a very common thing."

I Know What You Did Last Summer purports to be a morality tale about how a grave secret can come back to haunt you — even kill you. The cast, including Hewitt and Gellar (plus Freddie Prinze Jr. and Ryan Phillipe, who play their boyfriends), is young, hip, and gorgeous, and the soundtrack has a bunch of cool bands on it. But even though Williamson's protagonists are not the usual cardboard types (instead displaying vulnerability to all the weaknesses, fears, and humiliations of adolescence), this film is basically a straight rendition of the traditional teen horror movie, devoid of the unique genre-bending and wit of *Scream*, and completely lacking the pop-culture winks and MTV-generation irony that made that film so successful. Instead, *I Know What You Did* is a dull retread rather than something new. Although this was only his second produced film, it seemed Williamson had already lost his unique touch. But he would quickly regain it.

Sequels don't have to suck. You don't believe it? As evidence to the contrary you might offer the following: *Jaws 2*, *Godzilla Raids Again*, *Friday the 13th Part 3: 3-D*, *Son of Frankenstein*, *Speed 2*, *Batman and Robin*, *Lethal Weapon 4* . . . OK, you've got a point, but sequels don't *have* to suck. Kevin Williamson proved this with his next film, *Scream 2*, which, despite the fact that it was written and produced very quickly in order to capitalize on the momentum created by the original *Scream*, successfully rekindles the freshness of its predecessor without rehashing it to death, and adds a few new twists, turns, and scares of its own. In what might be construed as either the ultimate movie conceit or a brilliant plot device, Williamson and returning director Wes Craven meet the sequel jinx head-on, as the characters in *Scream 2* openly discuss the sequels that they think are better than their source material. During one heady classroom discussion, the kids note that *Terminator 2*, *Aliens*, and *Godfather 2* are, in their minds, superior to the films that inspired them. In another scene, Jamie Kennedy discusses how to make a successful horror sequel. He says, "The body count is always going to be bigger. The death scenes are always going to be more elaborate, and never assume the killer is dead, because he can always come back," and adds that the last rule of a sequel is that an actor must never accept less money than he was paid for the first film.

"The first movie was about high school students analyzing a horror film to catch a killer," Williamson said in an interview with the *Chicago Sun-Times* in December 1997. "Now it's film students analyzing horror film sequels to catch a copycat killer." In other words, it's the same nifty gimmick that infused *Scream* with a balance of scary gore and witty personality: when it comes to movies, these kids really know what they're talking about.

The sequel takes place two years after the events in *Scream*, and opens on a typical date night in an Ohio college town. In a notable Williamson/Cravenesque sequence that is both hilarious and gruesome, a young couple (Jada Pinkett and Omar Epps — as with Drew Barrymore in the first film, the early sacrificial lambs are played by familiar stars) attends a screening of the movie *Stab*, which is based on the Woodsboro murders and adapted from a nonfiction book by reporter Gale Weathers (Courteney Cox, reprising her role). In a promotional gimmick for *Stab*, the audience members wear freebie masks and hoods identical to those of the killer in the movie (and the movie-within-the-movie). In a dead-on parody of the con-

troversy over violence in horror flicks, the theater-goers are
worked into a frenzy, during which Epps and Pinkett are
brutally stabbed (he in the men's room, she in the theater), but
it's impossible to identify the killer because everyone's wearing
the same scary outfit. This sequence works equally well as an
incisive self-parody; *Stab* is a note-for-note replay of the events
in *Scream*, camped up in the style of a routine slasher pic; in
one of film's greatest in-jokes, the Drew Barrymore character is
played by Tori Spelling in *Stab*.

Meanwhile, across town, the kids who survived those
horrifying events in Woodsboro, California have graduated
from high school and now attend Windsor College in Ohio,
hoping to escape the terrible memories. They include Sidney
Prescott (Campbell), her cynical, video-geek friend Randy
(Jamie Kennedy), the cornball former Woodsboro deputy
Dewey Riley (David Arquette), and Cotton Weary (Liev
Schreiber, now playing a more prominent role), whom Sidney
accused of the murders before the duo of real psycho killers
were found out at the end of *Scream*. Sure enough, a copycat
killer shows up on campus and carves up students one by one,
prompting tabloid-queen newswoman Weathers to show up
for another scoop. In short order the killer or killers are
carving up the student body, striking at a sorority house, film
studios, camera vans, theaters, and so on. Between killings,
the killer phones several targets and taunts them with the
familiar refrain: "What's your favorite scary movie?" Before
long there is an impressive list of victims, and the movie
boasts a surprise ending.

It's an understatement to say that *Scream* and *Scream 2* recast the mold for modern teen horror pictures and raised the
bar for all future filmmakers taking a stab (pun intended) at
the genre. At the time they were released, these were the

smartest and most entertaining horror films to come along in a great while, but in the end, *Scream 2* doesn't have the first film's raison d'être and its own identity. While *Scream* was the ultimate riff on modern teen horror flicks, it left little in the way of uncharted territory to explore in future chapters. Audiences were mesmerized by *Scream's* blurring of the line between fiction and reality, and moviegoers were amused by director Craven and screenwriter Williamson's teasing ways — confronting the viewer with savage violence and mayhem, then pulling back and revealing that, after all, it's only a movie. *Scream 2* is infused with the same kind of tension between reality and perception; a few moments after a psychotic serial killer rips the guts out of a sweet teenage girl, the audiences is in stitches, laughing at another gag.

"We were more self-conscious about this picture," director Craven told the *Chicago Tribune* in 1997. "First of all, we didn't quite know what we had done right in the first one. . . . [One] thing we wanted to be acutely aware of was that there never be a moment that says to the audience, 'Aren't we so clever? Here we are, making our sequel.' Which was really tough because here you were, making jokes about sequels. But I was always looking for that point where there'd be one joke too much. There was a lot of attempted exercise in restraint."

Ultimately, however, *Scream 2* isn't quite as engaging as the original, partly because it treads familiar territory, partly because Williamson was forced to write the screenplay under pressure. In spring 1997, after *Scream's* incredible box-office success, Bob Weinstein (head of Miramax Films' Dimension Pictures division), decided he wanted a sequel for the upcoming holiday season. *Scream 2* was rushed into production at a time when Williamson was spread thin between *I Know What You Did Last Summer* and working on the pilot for *Dawson's Creek*. Williamson was still working on script revisions while the film was being shot, writing in a trailer on location in Atlanta. Plot details were kept top-secret from the press and public, and in order to enforce this code of silence (and, perhaps, because it simply wasn't finished yet), the screenplay was doled out to the actors in chunks; the ending of the movie and the identity of the killers was kept from the cast until the day it was shot.

With *Scream*, *I Know What You Did Last Summer*, and *Scream 2* igniting a renaissance in the subgenre known as slasher flicks, begetting a number of smart-aleck horror imitations (like *Urban Legend*, *Idle Hands*, and *Disturbing Behavior*), it was only natural that Hollywood would wind back the clock and revive the franchise that started it all, John Carpenter's *Halloween*. But the gap between the new breed of horror films with the self-aware humor that Williamson brought to the genre, and the relatively old-school approach taken by *Halloween* and the crop that followed it in the late 1970s and early 80s, is vast. Therefore, it is interesting that Williamson's original story for *Halloween: H20*, the seventh entry and 20th-anniversary film in the *Halloween* series, is a surprisingly straightforward, irony-free horror tale. And the film, directed by Stephen Miner (*Friday the 13th Part 3: 3-D*, *House*, *My Father the Hero*, *Lake Placid*), nobly tries to bring closure to the saga of "the shape," deranged killer Michael Myers, which had become entangled in a mess of loose ends over the course of several bad sequels. Williamson's story wisely throws all the inconsequential (and often boring) events of *Halloweens 4* through 6 by the wayside and the film is essentially a sequel to *Halloween 2*. For the uninitiated, Carpenter's *Halloween* is the story of a homicidal maniac who, in 1963, at age six, murdered one of his two sisters in Haddonfield, Illinois, and was then committed to a sanitarium. His parents died a few years later and the surviving sister, Laurie (Jamie Lee Curtis), was adopted by the Strode family. On Halloween night, 1978, Michael Myers broke out of the Smith's Grove Sanitarium and returned to Haddonfield, embarking on a killing spree and stalking his sister Laurie, who's making a few bucks babysitting some kids on trick-or-treat night. The events of that fateful evening were concluded in *Halloween 2*, which ended with Michael Myers, Laurie Strode, and Dr. Loomis (a psychologist studying Michael's mental illness, portrayed by Donald Pleasence) perishing in a hospital fire.

Of course, this being a horror movie, where no rules of mortality apply, none of them really died. In Kevin Williamson's revised *Halloween* universe, Laurie Strode became pregnant around 1980, faked her death in a car accident, took the phony name Keri Tate, had a son, and became a dean at a private school in tranquil Summer Glen, California. Dr. Loomis also survived the fire but eventually died in 1995 (however, had Donald Pleasence not really died, his character surely would have been resurrected, too). Most importantly, in spite of the fact that the last time he was seen in *Halloween 2* his body was engulfed in flames and he looked dead as a doornail, Michael Myers is alive and well, and he's apparently become one hell of a skip tracer. During a killing spree in Langdon, Illinois (sister Laurie's last known whereabouts), Michael finds clues as to his sister's new digs, jumps in an old beat-up 1970s clunker car and heads west, his old rubber Shatner mask not impairing his driving skills the least bit. Michael arrives on Halloween, just as most of the kids and faculty of Laurie's school are departing on a weekend trip, leaving the school deserted except for Laurie, her love interest (a teacher played by Adam Arkin), her son John (Josh Hartnett) and his girlfriend (Michelle Williams), and a few other kids. After 20 years, Michael Myers has come to settle the score with his sister: his intended victim is her teenage son. But even though there's a likable teenage ensemble and Myers respectably sends several of its members to grisly fates, this is really Kevin Williamson's first "adult" horror film, such as it is. At its center is the 20-year-long war of wills between Laurie Strode and her mass-murderer brother, a sibling rivalry pitting good versus evil, and Laurie's failure to escape a demon from the past that has sworn to follow her to the ends of the earth until she is eliminated. The greatest sequence of the film is the climactic confrontation between sister and slasher: instead of a typical teen murder-fest movie ending, in which the hapless victim is backed into a corner and must use her wits to somehow escape alive, Laurie grabs an ax, stalks back onto the grounds of the deserted campus where the "shape" is holed up, and shouts, "Michael!" into the dark night, challenging her bogeyman brother to a showdown.

While *Halloween: H20* didn't break ground the way *Scream* did, it nevertheless represents a milestone of sorts in horror movie history, the return of Jamie Lee Curtis to the genre, and the very movie that put her on the Hollywood map of stars' homes. Had it not been for *Halloween*, Curtis never would have become the scream queen of her generation, starring in films like *Prom Night*, *Terror Train*, and *The Fog*, nor likely would she have gone on to successes like *Trading Places*, *A Fish Called Wanda*, and *True Lies*. It's also cool that Williamson and Miner included a cameo role for Curtis's mother, Janet Leigh of Hitchcock's *Psycho* fame. "I asked Kevin Williamson to create a cameo for my mom that would give her the opportunity to tip her hat to *Psycho* and to acknowledge that she and I are horror icons," Curtis told the *Ottawa Sun* newspaper in 1998. Still, one question remains. What's with the "H20" in the title? Yes, it's a 20th anniversary movie, but "H20" seems to indicate the film takes place under water. In an appearance on ABC's *Good Morning America* in August 1998, Williamson explained, "we kept saying, you know, 'The posters should be H-20.' And then it just sort of [became] H2O, and the whole idea that, you know, Jamie Lee Curtis plays Laurie Strode, and they're brother and sister, her and the killer. And it's just sort of, 'blood is thicker than water.' She [Curtis] kind of liked that little tag line."

After the first three films he wrote grossed more than half a billion dollars worldwide, Kevin Williamson began receiving special considerations. The Weinsteins and Miramax gave him a $20-million development deal, locking up his next few screenplays, and they gave Williamson private flights aboard the Miramax jet. So, when a screenwriter is as successful as Kevin Williamson is, it's only a matter of time before some hotshot producer offers him a chance to direct a movie. It's Hollywood's way of keeping the golden boy happy. And so, in 1998, Bob Weinstein dangled *The Faculty* in front of Williamson's nose. *The Faculty*, a spoof of science-fiction films with a *Scream*-esque teenage ensemble, was Williamson's first departure from the slasher-movie genre, but it was not, as it turned out, his first job in the director's chair. "They [Miramax] said, 'This is right up your alley,'" Williamson said in a January 1999 interview with the *Chicago Sun-Times*. "So I got involved. . . . This was [*Invasion of the*] *Body Snatchers* meets *The Breakfast Club*. I started writing a draft of it, and the more I wrote, the more I was discovering the whole science-fiction world, which I don't know much about. I'm the horror/slasher guy."

However, as he delved deeper in to the story, which is about aliens invading the minds of the teachers at an Ohio high school, Williamson knew it was going to need lots of special effects in order to play out onscreen, and so he begged off the director's job, sticking to his trusty laptop instead. "I realized I didn't have a clue how to do this movie. It became apparent that this was probably not the best project with which to begin my directing career." Eventually, Williamson and others involved in the project decided they would pursue Robert Rodriguez, the director of such artfully violent pictures as *El Mariachi*, *Desperado*, and *From Dusk 'Till Dawn*, and one of the coolest young filmmakers in Hollywood. Over lunch at Roscoe's Chicken and Waffle, a soul-food joint in Hollywood, Williamson, Rodriguez, and Bob Weinstein (joined by Rodriguez's pal Quentin Tarantino) sealed the deal. Recalling the meeting, Rodriguez told the *Sun-Times*, "Bob said, 'We need a big Christmas movie. We need something to fill our traditional *Scream* slot, and this is the last Kevin script we've got. So you have to do it.'" *The Faculty* was the first production in a five-picture deal Rodriguez inked with Miramax.

The Faculty could have been called *My Teacher is an Alien*. At Herrington High School, in Ohio, the teachers succumb one by one to a hostile extraterrestrial invader that drains humans dry, literally, with each alien-infested teacher chugging bottles of water in order to survive. The epidemic gradually spreads to the students, their families, and the police. The day is saved by Zeke (Josh Hartnett), an underachiever student (he's repeating his senior year), who discovers that his homemade narcotic is deadly to the baddies. *The Faculty* features Williamson's by-now usual assortment of video-store references, and an amusing cast (particularly the actors playing teachers) that includes Piper Laurie, Jon Stewart, Bebe Neuwirth, and, in a cameo, the obese Internet movie-gossip guru Harry Knowles. But what's most interesting about this film is the lengths that Miramax went to promote it as a "Kevin Williamson movie," spending $30 million to market the film as such (by contrast, the film itself cost only $23 million to make) and paying $100,000 to the two screenwriters who penned the original script so they would agree to forfeit their writing credits. These behind-the-scenes maneuverings show just how much box-office power Williamson had amassed with only a few films under his belt.

The original draft of *The Faculty* was written by David Wechter and Bruce Kimmel, two Los Angeles low-budget film directors (Wechter made *Midnight Madness*, a 1980 film starring Michael J. Fox; Kimmel had directed *Spaceship*, a 1981 film with Leslie Nielsen), who sold it to Miramax for $225,000. But when Miramax became intent on advertising the film as "From the director of *Desperado*" with a "Screenplay by the writer of *Scream* & *Scream 2*," it became important to convince Wechter and Kimmel to surrender their story credits so that Williamson's name could stand alone. "We weren't trying to create something out of thin air," Mark Gill, president of Miramax Los Angeles, told the *Los Angeles Times* in January 1999. "When you have the opportunity to say your movie is from Kevin Williamson, it's an awfully potent marketing tool. Among under-25 moviegoers, the billing 'the writer of *Scream*' is a valuable calling card." For their part, the original screenwriters acknowledged that Williamson made significant changes to the script and they did not begrudge Miramax for distorting the truth when it implied in advertising hyperbole that Williamson had created the film. "He kept the basic story," Wechter told the *Los Angeles Times*, "but he rewrote all the dialogue, made the teenagers more hip and created several new characters. Our script had one main hero, but his version has a group of kids, which gives it more of a *Breakfast Club* feel."

When Kevin Williamson declined to direct *The Faculty*, the Weinsteins and Miramax were eager to find another project on which he could cut his filmmaking teeth; soon an agreement was made to resurrect his long-dormant screenplay *Killing Mrs. Tingle*, which had been languishing since he sold

Kevin Williamson and Katie Holmes at the premiere of *The Faculty*.

it three years before. Ultimately, it was a wise decision on both the studio's and Williamson's part to launch his directorial career with a relatively inexpensive, character-driven film rather than a big-budget, FX-laden affair, for Williamson stumbled awkwardly through his first picture, which was filmed in 1998 and released in August 1999 with the revised title *Teaching Mrs. Tingle*. The story, as discussed earlier, is Williamson's autobiographical tale of a sadistic high school teacher who is hypercritical of her students' work and revels in watching them fail. In the film, Katie Holmes of *Creek* fame plays Leigh Ann, a straight-A student and the daughter of a hard-working waitress (Leslie Ann Warren, who keeps falling asleep with burning cigarettes in her hand for some unknown reason), who's striving to become her high school's valedictorian so she can land a scholarship to some unnamed college. Standing in her way is the titular Mrs. Tingle, a hard-ass history teacher who openly belittles her students with sadistic glee. Leigh Ann takes great pains to pass her history final by re-creating the diary of a woman accused at the Salem witch trials — not only does she write the huge memoir, but also binds it in a leather sleeve and ages the paper for authenticity! Still, it's not enough to impress that bitch Tingle, who gives the girl a "C," threatening to derail her academic future. Things get out of hand when a hunky-but-stupid boy named Luke (Barry Watson of TV's *Seventh Heaven*), whom Leigh and her best gal-pal Jo Lynn (Marisa Coughlan of Williamson's other TV series, *Wasteland*) both have their hormones set on, steals the answers to Mrs. Tingle's final exam; before the righteous Leigh Ann can convince the dufus Luke to return the cheat-sheet, Mrs. Tingle catches the three kids with the answers and plans to report the incident to the principal the following morning. That night, the trio of friends visits Mrs. Tingle at her southern gothic home in hopes of setting the record straight, but a scuffle ensues and Mrs. Tingle is rendered unconscious with a crossbow (don't ask). From this point forward, the three kids do absolutely nothing right or realistic: they take Mrs. Tingle hostage in her own home, tying her to the bed, hand-feeding her fast food ("you want ketchup on your fries, Mrs. Tingle?" Luke asks — really), and blackmailing her with nasty photos in hopes she'll drop the whole thing and give the kids good grades. The climax is equally as stupid as the rest of the film.

Forget all of Williamson's past successes. *Teaching Mrs. Tingle* is a stupefying movie — stupefying because, at its center, the story possesses much potential, little of which is ever realized. With all of its absurd situations and actions, Williamson's script begs to be treated as a comic satire, but as a director he seems unable to appreciate the dark humor in his own script! Thus, patently farcical situations (like Mrs. Tingle tied up on her bed, her arms outstretched and tied to the bedpost, in a crucifixion-like image) are played absolutely straight; the only successful attempt at humor comes in the form of another typical Williamson riff, a writhing tribute to Linda Blair's possession in *The Exorcist* performed by Coughlin's character, a ditzy young actress type. Meanwhile, the entire film is backed by the same sort of easily digestible alternative-music soundtrack that is fine for the soap-opera goings-on of a *Dawson's Creek* episode, but seems completely inappropriate for a film about three selfish teens who shame-lessly break a series of criminal laws, and learn absolutely nothing in the process except that the most important thing in life is to come out on top, no matter whom you must tread over to get there. Throughout the movie, there is a running dialogue between Tingle and her students about the meaning of the word "irony"; it seems that Williamson should have looked it up in Webster's, too. *Teaching Mrs. Tingle* is not a terrible film; in fact, the performances of British actress Helen Mirren as the tormenting educator and Marisa Coughlin (whose comic timing is excellent) are among the bright spots, and Williamson makes a nice wink to his favorite John Hughes movies by casting Molly Ringwald as a dim-witted office girl moonlighting as a substitute teacher. But the film is terribly misguided, and the fact that such a snide piece of work could come from a writer whose previous movies tempered their smarminess with a dose of humanity is something of a letdown.

As noted previously, the original title of this film was *Killing Mrs. Tingle*. In May 1999, just one month after two Columbine High School students staged a massacre on their Littleton, Colorado, campus and killed 15 students and teachers, Miramax Films announced that it would redub Williamson's then-forthcoming film *Teaching Mrs. Tingle*. Miramax officials insisted the change had nothing to do with the recent campus killings, which were covered by news media around the world and shocked the nation. "These students will do everything they can to avoid killing Mrs. Tingle . . . nobody dies in the movie," a Miramax official said, "We have been looking for another title for a long time." Why the studio felt it necessary to deny that the title change had anything to do with the Columbine tragedy is unknown, but even Williamson himself chimed in, claiming that the title change was his idea. "When you have Kevin Williamson associated with a movie with 'killing' in the title, everyone's gonna think it's a horror movie," he told *Time Out New York* magazine. "And that bugged me, because this is my opportunity to not make a horror movie — to make something different." Which begs the question: if the title is so inappropriate, why didn't he call it *Teaching Mrs. Tingle* from the start, when he wrote it several years earlier? The name change, and Miramax's attempt to distance the film from the Columbine massacre, also prompted the usual questions from the media as to whether movie violence triggers real-life murder — a suggestion that Williamson has always flatly refuted. The prior year, when the release of *Scream 2* was delayed in Japan due to a student's grisly decapitation at a Kyoto school, Williamson told the *Japan Times*, "Movies don't create violence in any way, shape or form . . . I can sit here till the cows come home and tell you that movies don't cause violence, but you say that to the victim's family and you might get a different response."

Teaching Mrs. Tingle was a box-office flop; within two weeks of its release in major U.S. cities it had pretty much faded from the local cinemas. But it hardly spelled the end of Williamson's career. By the time Tingle was released, he was already preparing his next feature film, *Her Leading Man* (written by *Dawson's Creek* co-producer Greg Berlanti), which was due to be released in 2000, and in which Williamson promised to do for the romantic comedy what *Scream* did for teen horror. In 1998 he told the *Orange County Register*, "I'm really sick of the romantic-comedy genre. I do so want to attack that genre to see if there's anything left to tell." *Her Leading Man*, he later told the *London Daily Telegraph*, is an attempt "to do everything people love about a romantic comedy, and not make them hate themselves for loving it." But, at the same time, Williamson began to slow his once-hectic writing pace. Just as he withdrew himself from the responsibility of writing *Dawson's Creek* in the show's second season, Williamson found it necessary for his health and sanity to drop out of *Scream 3*. Although he had written a draft of the story, he asked Miramax's Bob Weinstein if he could bow out of the script-writing assignment, and Weinstein was sympathetic. "I've got to slow down, or I'm never going to live to see a long-term career," Williamson told *The Advocate*. Eventually, the *Scream 3* screenplay was written by Ehren Kruger; the story — which was once again kept top-secret during filming — reportedly takes place on the set of *Stab 2* (another movie within a movie), where all of the actors start getting killed. Will Williamson return to the slasher genre? It doesn't seem as though he's eager to. As far back as 1997, when *Scream 2* was released, he told the *San Francisco Chronicle* that after finishing *Scream 3* (which he was already committed to write) he'd quit the genre. "The best part is that after *Scream 3* I don't have to write any more horror movies," he said. "I think I've done horror movies, and I want to move on and not make another one as long as I live."

AT THE ALTAR OF SPIELBERG

Kevin Williamson has cited several key influences on his writing style, among them directors John Carpenter and John Hughes. But the artistic lens through which Williamson views his universe is modeled after the viewfinder on Steven Spielberg's Arriflex camera. More than anyone or anything, it is Spielberg and his work that has shaped Williamson's fantasy-world view and informed his screenplays. "I'm in this business because of him, Spielberg," Williamson said in an interview with the *Orange County Register* in 1998. "He's answered what I'll spend the rest of my life doing. Spielberg is quite simply the greatest filmmaker of my time. He has made so many movies that are about abandonment, like *E.T.*, where E.T. was separated from his mother. It's very universal and very related to a young audience. And if you look at Spielberg's early career, basically Dawson is following it. He wants his life to be like the movies, which is where his idealism comes from."

Williamson has never attempted to emulate or imitate his idol; his screenplays are relatively small-scale affairs in comparison to Spielberg's body of work (which includes American epics like *Jaws*, *Close Encounters*, *Raiders of the Lost Ark*, *E.T.*, *Schindler's List*, *Saving Private Ryan*, and so on). The characters and the dramatic terrain covered in Williamson's film and TV work is also decidedly more cynical, and infused with that edgy, 1990s self-awareness, whereas Spielberg's world has always been a somewhat naïve place, where optimism and honor reign and sentimentalism is not taboo. Williamson ingeniously finds a middle ground between the contemporary kids of his media-savvy/movie-encyclopedic/sex-obsessed/modern universe and Spielberg's idealism in *Dawson's Creek* by instilling Dawson Leery with a sense of Spielbergian purity. Dawson is 15 years going on middle age, an aspiring filmmaker who is wise beyond his years, and who decorates his room with Spielberg movie posters, arranged in order of each film's box-office performance. Dawson is the show's moral center, a young man struggling to find his identity in a small-town world where innocence is lost faster and faster at a younger and younger age. In a sense, it's a terribly contrived device — in recent years, it has become fashionable among film critics to discount the importance of Spielberg's work, which has grown increasingly sappy; not only that, the young people of today undoubtedly relate better to young, hip, and more hard-edged directors like Quentin Tarantino, Kevin Smith (*Clerks*, *Dogma*), or pretentious "indie" talents like Harmony Korine (*Kids*, *Gummo*) or Todd Solondz (*Welcome to the Dollhouse*, *Happiness*). But perhaps the premise works because it lends Dawson a sense of chivalry; while his friend Pacey is living the ultimate adolescent fantasy — a sexual affair with his 30-something teacher — or when he finds out his mother is having an affair, Dawson puts his trust and faith in the god Spielberg.

"In *Dawson's Creek*, when a girl and her boyfriend have a fight, she tells him, 'Look, even Steven Spielberg outgrew his Peter Pan syndrome.' Well, to me, that has just as much emotional resonance as anything you'd hear in *Little House on the Prairie*," Williamson explained to the *Los Angeles Times*. The world of *Dawson's Creek*, he contends, is a mirror of the real world. "When we sit down at the table at home, what do we discuss? Movies and TV," he added in another interview. "In other TV shows, we ignore that movies and TV exist. Not my kids in *Dawson's*. When something happens, I love their references because they help tell the story." Just like the characters in the *Scream* movies (and, incidentally, like one of the guys in Kevin Smith's *Clerks*, another movie that serves as a postmodern, pop-culture reference guide), Pacey and Dawson work in a video rental store, which provides the backdrop for much of their film-speak.

Unfashionable as it might be, Williamson is unabashed in his praise of Spielberg. In 1998, an interviewer who visited Williamson's offices in West Hollywood noted that the only book there was one of two recent Spielberg biographies, and Williamson said he had the other one at home, by his bedside. To be fair, though, Spielberg isn't the only inspiration for the show. Williamson relates that his original idea was to do an updated version of *James at 15*, an excellent NBC drama that premiered in 1977 and starred Lance Kerwin (*The Loneliest Runner*) as James Hunter, a kid who moved with his family from Oregon to Boston and had to deal with coming-of-age issues in a new, big-city setting. There are several similarities between the two shows — for instance, while Dawson wants to make movies, James was a budding photographer — and both shows tackled provocative issues like sex, fidelity, drugs, and parental relationships, although *Dawson's Creek* is obviously much more frank than *James at 15* ever could be.

Williamson also was inspired by *My So-Called Life*, the 1994–95 ABC drama starring Claire Danes as an introspective teen. But then, Williamson is a pop-culture sponge, taking material from innumerable sources. "To my generation, pop culture is everything. When I sit down to write, I don't think, how many pop culture references can I fit in? The characters are just like me, they relate life to the movies," he said.

THE GAY NINETIES

OK, so it wasn't as if Brad Pitt or Richard Gere or the Backstreet Boys had come out of the closet; screenwriters, after all, aren't commonly thought of as heartthrobs by pubescent little girls. And, in the late 1990s, public proclamations of homosexuality by celebrities, while still somewhat infrequent, aren't necessarily earth-shattering anymore (unless, of course, you're Brad Pitt, Richard Gere, or the Backstreet Boys). But there undoubtedly were a few females out there who were dismayed when, in February 1999, Kevin Williamson told the world he is gay.

The big news (ho-hum) came out, not coincidentally, at the same time that Jack McPhee (Kerr Smith) did the same thing on *Dawson's Creek*, in an episode that aired February 17, 1999. It wasn't the first time a prime-time television character had come out of the closet (Ellen DeGeneres famously broke that taboo when her character did the same thing on the sitcom *Ellen*, during the 1997–98 season), but it *was* the first time it happened on a TV show specifically aimed at young audiences. Williamson, who has always said that *Creek* is an autobiographical show — with each of its characters representing some facet of his own life — was quick to add, however, that Jack's inner battles with anxiety and confusion over his sexual identity, and his outer battles with homophobia in the Capeside community, are not taken from his own diaries. In fact, Williamson told the *New York Daily News*, "I was welcomed with open arms by my parents" when he broke the news to them. Williamson claims he has always been open about his sexuality, but before Jack began to deal with such issues on the show, no one had really bothered to ask him about it (after all, how many times have interviewers asked Woody Allen or Joe Eszterhas or Shane Black or Robert Towne if they were gay?). As to why he never brought it up before, Williamson told the *Daily News*, "I don't see where I serve myself, or anyone else, to scream at the top of my lungs that I'm gay."

Williamson's public coming-out was soon followed by a cover story about him in the gay community's magazine, *The Advocate*, which called him "the most successful openly gay hyphenate in Hollywood." As to why he outed himself, Williamson told the magazine, "I just reached a point where [I thought], I'm gay, I've told my parents, all my friends, everybody I know knows I'm gay." Williamson says he knew he was gay since his adolescence but kept quiet about it because of his Bible Belt surroundings and Southern Baptist upbringing. As a youngster, he endured the local preacher's Sunday fire-and-brimstone sermons, some of which condemned homosexuals to the same hellish fate as rapists and murderers, he said. For the sake of appearances, Williamson dated a girl named Fannie, his best friend throughout high school and college, before moving to New York to become an actor. Then, after moving to Los Angeles, he finally made peace with himself and accepted his own sexuality. But the toughest part was breaking the news to his parents, whom he told during a 1992 trip home to North Carolina. Both parents accepted the news, saying, "'It doesn't matter what you are or who you are,'" Williamson said in the *Advocate* interview. In the years since, Williamson has grown closer to his father, with whom he'd had a distant relationship prior to coming out; in fact, when Williamson was conducting research for the *I Know What You Did Last Summer* script, his dad took him out on the boat and acted as unofficial "fisherman consultant." Williamson even wanted to name the film's hook-handed killer after his pop (who approved), but the studio heads wouldn't allow it.

It took a while for Williamson's sexuality to reveal itself in his work. There are no gay characters in his first three films, *Scream*, *I Know What You Did Last Summer* and *Scream 2*, but after some prodding by Ellen DeGeneres (who was living across the street from him at the time), he became convinced he should use his position in the entertainment business to set an example for gay youth. Thus came, in February 1998, Jack McPhee's startling revelation on *Dawson's Creek*, along with Williamson's real-life disclosure. The revelation made no great tremors on the social landscape, although the usual opponents on both sides of the gay-rights debate voiced their opinions. "We love it," Scott Seomin, spokesman for the gay-rights group GLAAD (Gay and Lesbian Alliance Against Defamation), told the *Arkansas Democrat-Gazette* newspaper. "It's important for a couple of reasons. This is an age when people can be so confused about who they are sexually and, while we're seeing more gay images on television, we're not seeing people struggle with it." On the other side of the fence, Brent Bozell III, chairman of the conservative Parents Television Council, said, "There is very much an agenda in Hollywood to advance the cause of homosexuality as normal behavior by making those who think otherwise the deviants." Referring to Tyson, Dawson Leery's fundamentalist Christian friend, who objected to Jack's coming-out and was verbally thrashed for it, Bozell said, "a character can put forward an argument, but you can be sure it's a character who moonlights as a troglodyte."

Williamson promised that in future episodes of *Dawson's Creek*, Jack McPhee would continue to struggle with his sexuality in front of prime-time viewers; in fact, Jack was to begin dating guys during the show's second season. And Williamson has already shown a commitment to finding roles for gay characters in his universe: the TV drama *Wasteland* (which premiered on the ABC network in the 1999–2000 season) features actor Dan Montgomery as Russell Bass, a soap opera actor living in the closet, and his film *Her Leading Man* (scheduled for release in 2000) includes a gay screenwriter as a prominent character. Williamson may not be the loudest voice for gay rights in Hollywood, but in his own, quiet way he hopes to help give a voice to young gays and lesbians in his work. "I don't think I'm the right person to be on the soapbox," he told *The Advocate*, "but if I . . . can talk openly about [his sexuality] and it helps anybody, then my job is done."

FOREVER YOUNG

Never trust anyone over 30, the old saying goes. But the kids of today trust Kevin Williamson, even though he was 31 by the time he had his first hit with *Scream*. His secret? He takes that old "never trust anyone . . ." maxim and makes it his own: his characters are savvy teens with more common sense than their parents, teachers, and other authority figures. It's not always realistic, but the kids in Kevin's world have an elevated emotional maturity and social conscience reminiscent of the self-righteous teens in John Hughes movies, but jaded with what Williamson terms the "earlier-than-ever disappointment factor." Everyone remembers, he says, the first time that a

parent or authority figure profoundly disappointed them —
catching mom in bed with the milkman, dad stumbling home
drunk, etc. "It's the moment when you first realize that your
parents are human beings, too," Williamson told the *Boston
Globe* in 1997. "For me and my generation, the age when that
happened might have come in the mid-to-late teens. With the
kids today, it happened when they were seven or eight or nine.
I don't think it's a coincidence that many of my teen characters
talk in this psychobabble language, that they analyze
themselves and the situations they or others are in, as if
they've been in therapy themselves for seven years. And I
think the kids watching relate to that on a level most of us
don't fully appreciate." This theme of trust — in particular, the
untrustworthiness of the average adult — is at the center of
every episode of *Dawson's Creek*. The parents, teachers, and
other mentor figures of *Dawson's* are not portrayed in the most
favorable light — it's a world where the Eddie Haskells are
always smarter than the Cleaver families and, in this case,
more upstanding, too. So, Dawson Leery counsels his
emotionally immature mom, forcing her to admit her
infidelity to his dad. Dawson, not the show's adults, is the
barometer of moral decency and social decorum — when he
walks into a room and finds his parents heatedly getting it on,
he's not glad his folks are still virile, but instead, is disgusted
at their vulgar display.

Williamson also connects to teens on another level: even
though he's well into his thirties, he still can remember the
emotional rollercoaster that is adolescence. Most adults, he
says, forget what it's like to be 14 or 15, and therein lies the
generation gap. "As adults, we try to achieve a balance in our
lives," Williamson told the *Boston Globe*. "We don't usually
have the intense highs and lows. But as a 15-year-old, it's all

about highs and lows. There is no balance, no perspective, because that's all you know. So you're looking for an adrenaline rush to play into or get those highs going for you. Kids need to do something with those raging hormones, and a horror movie is like a roller-coaster ride, and it can do that for you. I understand that; I still think of myself as a kid." For some reason, Williamson has a particular insight into the hearts and minds of teenage girls, as evidenced by the abundance of strong, young female roles he has created both for *Dawson's Creek* and his films — roles which have helped surge the career of several actresses now known as bankable commodities, including not only Katie Holmes and Michelle Williams but also Sarah Michelle Gellar, Marisa Coughlan, Neve Campbell, and Rebecca Gayheart. And these actresses will vouch for his ability to write believable teens. "Kevin talks to teenagers at their level instead of talking down to them," Gellar told the *Milwaukee Journal Sentinel* in 1997. "He's like a teenager. He's a big kid. He's a big smart kid."

Dawson's Creek was patterned after Kevin Williamson's southern-fried formative years. Although he has promised he will "never be far" from the show, fans will be watching to see how far it strays, in its third season, from Williamson's prototype. Why? As mentioned earlier, in 1999, Williamson relinquished all his duties as a writer and executive producer on the show in order to concentrate on his new TV series, *Wasteland*, which is inspired by his aimless, 20-something, post-college years when he lived in New York. Around the same time, he also dropped himself from the *Scream 3* project. After three years of overworking himself, and after a three-year romance crashed and burned, Williamson said he was feeling the stress catch up to him and he needed to cut back his workload to avoid going insane. It seems, after three years of non-stop teen culture, Kevin Williamson was finally starting to grow up — something he has always resisted. "I don't consider myself an adult yet, so maybe some of these answers about these bigger issues will come," he told the *Toronto Sun* in summer 1998. "I'll reach an answer when I continue to evolve. I'm a work in progress."

KEVIN WILLIAMSON'S CREDITS

Films: *Scream* (screenwriter), released December 20, 1996; *I Know What You Did Last Summer* (screenwriter), released October 17, 1997; *Scream 2* (screenwriter, executive producer), released December 12, 1997; *Halloween H20* (original story, co-executive producer), released August 5, 1998; *The Faculty* (screenwriter), released December 25, 1998; *Teaching Mrs. Tingle* (screenwriter, director), released August 20, 1999; *Scream 3* (original story, producer), released December 10, 1999; *Her Leading Man* (director), to be released in 2000.

Television: *Dawson's Creek* (creator, executive producer), premiered January 20, 1998; *Wasteland* (creator, executive producer), premiered October 7, 1999.

CHAPTER SOURCES

"And one to grow on; the scaremeister who brought us *Scream* has turned his attention to a new TV show about teenagers." *St. Louis Post-Dispatch.* January 20, 1998.

Chadwick, Alan. "Hollywood Hotshot." *The London Sunday Times.* November 23, 1997.

Chanko, Kenneth M. "He knows what scares us." *Boston Globe.* November 30, 1997.

Covert, Colin. "Revenge is sweet for *Scream* writer." Minneapolis *Star Tribune.* December 14, 1997.

Curtis, Quentin. "A Spielberg for the next generation; Kevin Williamson's way with teen audiences has made him Hollywood's hottest writer." *London Daily Telegraph*. May 8, 1998.

Dudek, Duane. "A (scary) teenager at heart." *Milwaukee Journal Sentinel*. December 14, 1997.

Emmanuel, Greg. "Revenge of the words." *Time Out New York*. August 19-26, 1999.

Epstein, Jeffrey. "Kevin Williamson unbound." *The Advocate*. August 31, 1999.

Fretts, Bruce. "High school confidential: Dawson's Creek." *Entertainment Weekly Online*. Online. January 1998.

Goldstein, Patrick. "Screamwriter; Kevin Williamson, the pied piper of the video generation, has breathed new life into the teen horror genre." *Los Angeles Times*. October 27, 1997.

Goldstein, Patrick. "A creative spin on hardball PR game." *Los Angeles Times*. January 1, 1999.

"Halloween scream-writer." *Good Morning America*. August 4, 1998.

Hobson, Louis B. "Queen of scream returns." *The Ottawa Sun*. August 2, 1998.

"Hormones rage in Dawson's Creek." *Denver Rocky Mountain News*. January 18, 1998.

Houpt, Simon. "A screaming success with the teen crowd." *Globe and Mail*. August 14, 1999.

Jicha, Tom. "Young WB has young pair of aces." *Fort Lauderdale Sun-Sentinel*. January 11, 1999.

Lee, Yishane. "Writer takes a stab at deconstruction." *The Japan Times*. August 18, 1998.

Littlefield, Kinney. "Drama's creator is addicted to adolescence." *Orange County Register*. January 18, 1998.

Mooney, Joshua. "*Scream* writer turns to sci-fi." *Chicago Sun-Times*. January 1, 1999.

Murray, Steve. "*Scream* writer's secret weapon: ear for south." *Chicago Tribune*. December 21, 1997.

Pearlman, Cindy. "*Scream* gem; but who's the killer?" *Chicago Sun-Times*. December 7, 1997.

Stack, Peter. "Screenwriter's slice of life." *San Francisco Chronicle*. December 13, 1997.

Strauss, Bob. "Scary thought: Wes Craven not making a horror picture? That's exactly what's going to happen." *Los Angeles Daily News*. December 25, 1997.

"Teen tongues wagging over Dawson's Creek; Scream writer creates spicy WB series." *The Atlanta Journal and Constitution*. January 12, 1998.

Tucker, Ken, Wanda Wertheimer, Robert Siegel, hosts. "*Dawson's Creek*." *All Things Considered*. National Public Radio. January 20, 1998.

THE IMPORTANCE OF
BEING EARNEST

TV TEENS IN THE 1990S

In the final years of the 20th century there was an unprecedented youth boom in American popular culture. It is hard to pinpoint exactly when it happened, but sometime in the mid-1990s, the teenage children of the Baby Boomers came of age — the age of mass-market consumption, that is — forming the largest audience of teens in American history, and with the U.S. economy in good shape, these kids had money to burn. Those entertainment mavens in Hollywood who were quick to smell the scent of young money cashed in by creating a fresh new crop of teen idols in all arenas of pop media. The music industry had Fiona Apple, Hanson, The Backstreet Boys, and Britney Spears; television gave us Neve Campbell, Jennifer Love Hewitt, and Sarah Michelle Gellar; and the movies had, well, Neve Campbell, Jennifer Love Hewitt, and Sarah Michelle Gellar. Of course, this was hardly the first such craze in Hollywood; teen entertainment, like everything else, is cyclical. What was different about 1990s-style teen pop fodder was the age of the audience. In the past, "young" TV viewers were described as between ages 18 and 34; now it was between the adolescent years of 12 and 17. Suddenly, on the television front, networks and their advertisers were keen on reaching millions of kids in this hormonally active age group, particularly the girls, who were said to watch any program with attractive actors who look like teens (note the term "look like"). As Puff Daddy said, "it's all about the Benjamins." It was into this market-driven TV land that *Dawson's Creek* was born in January 1998.

But first, rewind back to the late 1980s. The Reagan Era. The "Me" Decade. The bloated defense industry helps to falsely inflate the nation's economy, and the dividing line between haves and have-nots becomes wider and wider. What a time to be a teen — across the suburban wasteland, high school students with engineers for dads are driving BMWs to school and wearing Lacoste and Polo; those with working-stiff parents are taking the bus and wearing hand-me-downs. Director John Hughes took teen class warfare and other angst-ridden issues to heart in films like *The Breakfast Club*, *Pretty in Pink*, and *Some Kind of Wonderful* — the movies usually cited as the best representation of what it was like to grow into adulthood during this very superficial, materialistic decade. However, that distinction really goes to Amy Heckerling's *Fast Times at Ridgemont High*, a film usually mistaken for a simple comedy because of Sean Penn's silly role as Jeff Spicoli, the surfer-stoner. This film is a frank portrayal of teen life in middle America — dumb jobs at the mall, first loves, losing your virginity, teen pregnancy, abortion, masturbation, and so on. Sound familiar? *Dawson's Creek* creator Kevin Williamson may pay lip service to John Hughes, and there are definite similarities between the angst-addled, parent-blaming kids stuck in after-school detention in *The Breakfast Club* and their counterparts stuck in Capeside, but Williamson's teens also owe more than a passing glance to Mark "Rat" Ratner, Stacy, Brad, Mike Damone, and the other kids in *Fast Times*.

By the early 1990s, John Hughes and his idyllic teen world (usually set in suburban Chicago) were history. So were most of the 1980s teen idols, like Anthony Michael Hall, Debbie Gibson, and Tiffany. Then Nirvana's *Nevermind* album exploded into a huge hit, and awakened the entertainment and advertising industries to a whole new breed of youth, the downcast slacker; pretty soon, everyone was detuning their guitars and singing off-key, and The Gap was selling flannel shirts. The kids born between the mid-1960s and the mid-1970s were quickly labeled "Generation X" (hey, it sounded cool at the time) and exploited for a few years. The prevailing image of teens on television, however, was quite different from the scruffy scraps hanging out at the record store at the time. In 1990, the upstart Fox Television Network carved its own unique niche in the broadcasting marketplace when it launched *Beverly Hills, 90210*, the legendary prime-time soap about a group of teen friends living in a well-to-do Los Angeles suburb once home to the Clampetts. The show, created by Aaron Spelling — the producer who brought such entertainment milestones as *Charlie's Angels* to the world — gave Fox its own identity as the "youth network," made sideburns fashionable again and made stars out of young actors like Jason Priestley, Luke Perry, Shannen Doherty, and Tori Spelling. Created in the pop-culture gap between the self-absorbed 1980s and the self-aware 1990s, *Beverly Hills, 90210* was the first prime-time drama to depict teens confronting adult problems without resorting to authority figures for the answers; it bridged the gap between the last wave of Gen-X kids and the current wave of teens who are growing up in a more fast-paced, digitally deflowered world.

Nevertheless, there is a huge difference between the *90210* phenomenon and the teen wave that begot *Dawson's Creek*. While Jason Priestley et al. were bona fide stars in their day, their popularity was limited to TV (and, in Doherty's case, her cat-fights at the Roxbury night club); the few movies that starred the *90210* kids bombed (can you name one?). Brian Austin Green made a rap album and it, too, tanked. But the *Dawson's* gang are taking their popularity all the way to the Bank of Hollywood — within a few months after the show debuted, all four principal cast members were starring in major motion pictures, and their compatriots from the other popular teen shows of the day, like *Party of Five* and *7th Heaven* were doing the same. So, what happened? Why is the late-90s teen boom a full-fledged, cash-cow industry, whereas the early-90s wave was merely a phenomenon?

Two words: The Demographic.

Somewhere along the way, a clever person in Hollywood must have read some statistics from the U.S. Census Bureau and discovered that, as of the mid-1990s, there were some 37 million kids between the ages of 10 and 19; looking further, they would have found that the government expected that number to increase to 42 million by 2005. Studies estimated that these teens wielded more than $80 million in disposable income each year and — compared to those old farts in the over-20 age group — these kids were going to the movies more, buying more CDs, renting more videos, watching more TV, spending more time on the Internet — in short, they were an untapped goldmine for the entertainment mavens. Someone also must have noticed that these kids were a different breed than the mopey slacker types that the media was paying so much attention to just a few years ago; the new teens are more communicative and open-hearted, if not exactly optimistic about the future. They are also a more savvy, media-aware, ambitious, and pragmatic bunch — where their predecessors worked at burger stands, these youths were mastering the Internet and getting ready to launch multimillion-dollar IPOs just a few years down the road; they are more apt to deal with problems rather than just ignore

them or lash out irrationally, like when Christian Slater tried
to blow up his school in the movie *Heathers*. For these teens,
reality doesn't bite, it just stings a little. And so, when the
powers that be in television, film, and the music business set
about confiscating the allowances and after-school incomes of
these new kids, they set about creating teen images of sincerity
and self-awareness. Can somebody say "Hanson?"

The youth boom didn't happen all at once, especially on
the TV front. One of the first shows to exemplify the New
Earnestness of the 1990s teen was *My So-Called Life*, which
starred a young Claire Danes and ran for one low-rated season
on ABC in 1994. Undoubtedly, however, *My So-Called Life*
(which, just a few years later, was resurrected in well-rated
reruns on MTV) paved the way for Fox's *Party of Five*, which
followed one year later and became a great success. Unlike
other recent teen shows like *90210* in which teen problems
were usually remedied or at least sorted out by the end of a
one-hour episode, *Party of Five* (which depicted the ongoing
saga of the orphaned Salinger siblings) was a quality drama in
which struggles of love and life were more realistically
portrayed as protracted problems. *Party of Five* fandom also
reached unprecedented levels — its stars not only were feted
on popular television talk shows, but the now-blooming
Internet age gave rise to dozens of fan Web sites lauding the
show and its individual stars, and fans gathered in Internet
chat rooms to chew the fat on the latest episode. The show
also set a precedent as *all* of its stars — Scott Wolf, Neve
Campbell, Jennifer Love Hewitt, Matthew Fox, and Lacey
Chabert — became teen idols, and many of them eventually
crossed over into successful film careers (something that few
TV teen stars had managed since John Travolta broke out of
Welcome Back, Kotter for *Saturday Night Fever* nearly 20 years
before). Around the same time, teens were becoming big

business on the big screen: in 1995, Amy Heckerling's comedy *Clueless* grossed $57 million and made a star out of 15-year-old Alicia Silverstone; and a TV kid named Leonardo DiCaprio, who had appeared on the sitcom *Growing Pains* in the early 1990s, was also forcing Hollywood to take note of the under-20 set as he made girls swoon in movies like the hipper-than-thou *William Shakespeare's Romeo & Juliet*, released in 1996.

Suddenly, the demand for teen movies and television shows seemed to explode; among the movies that followed were two neo-slasher pictures called *Scream* (1996) and *I Know What You Did Last Summer* (1997), both of which starred *Party of Five*'s resident ingenues (Neve Campbell in *Scream*, Jennifer Love Hewitt in *I Know . . .*) and both of which were written by a hot new screenwriter named Kevin Williamson, who had a flair for putting catchy dialogue in the mouths of babes. After *Scream* grossed more than $100 million for Miramax Films, Williamson was being approached by numerous Hollywood studios coveting his pen, most of them offering him big bucks to write yet another scary movie. But Williamson was already looking to expand his dramatic horizons; so, while many TV writers longed to make the transition to big-screen projects, Williamson did exactly the opposite and went from writing movies to creating a television show. He had a rough idea for a semi-autobiographical teen drama series, which he pitched to several networks including Fox, where the idea men said it was too similar to the then-struggling *Party of Five*, and rejected it. Finally Williamson presented his concept to the fledgling Warner Bros. Television Network (known in the biz by the moniker "the WB"). "I was making it up as I pitched it," he later remembered. In early 1997, the WB signed Williamson and Columbia TriStar Television to develop *Dawson's Creek*, which the writer proudly boasted, "has no horror element to it at all. . . . It's *Kids* meets *Little House on the Prairie*. It's both sweet but very contemporary and provocative, since we're talking about teens today."

Dawson's Creek fit perfectly into the WB's youth-oriented game plan. The WB made its debut on American airwaves in January 1995 and, from the beginning, it emulated the formulas that had enabled the Fox Network to compete with the big three of ABC, CBS, and NBC beginning in the late 1980s. It was no coincidence — the WB was run by Jamie Kellner, who had formerly been head of Fox, and its chief programming executive, Garth Ancier, had previously held the same title at Fox (Ancier left the WB a few years later). Because of heated competition with Paramount's UPN Network, which made its broadcasting debut at roughly the same time, the WB was forced to carve its programming niche quickly. Initially, both the WB and UPN relied heavily on comedies targeting African-Americans and urban audiences, like *The Wayans Bros.* and *The Parent 'Hood*; that formula didn't last long, however, and soon the WB was retooling, adding programming for kids like Steven Spielberg's animated *Animaniacs* and, more significantly, teen programs, the first of which was *Buffy the Vampire Slayer*, which debuted in 1997 as a midseason replacement. Inspired by a movie of the same name, which in 1992 tanked at the box office and then became a cult fave on home video, *Buffy* stars teen ex-soap opera actress Sarah Michelle Gellar as the titular undead-killer, who kick-boxes vampires, witches, and giant bugs, delivering witty one-liners in the process. Described by *Entertainment Weekly* as "part X-Files*, part *Heathers*, part *Xena*," *Buffy* is the brainchild of Joss Whedon who, like Kevin Williamson, was first a successful screenwriter (he wrote the movie version of *Buffy*, *Toy Story*, and was a script doctor on *Speed*), and was writing teen material well into his thirties. *Buffy* quickly became a major hit for the WB and, according to some reports, single-handedly

The cast of *Dawson's Creek* meets Sarah Michelle Gellar and Nicholas Brendon of *Buffy* fame.

saved the struggling network from oblivion by pulling in real-life ratings and ad revenues.

Explaining the show's success, Whedon told *Entertainment Weekly*, "Teenagers today have really keen bullshit detectors. They can smell a lie like a fart in a car." *Buffy* signaled to the WB that cutting-edge teen programming — the kind with sex, attitude, and good looks to spare — was a niche to be carved. So, when Williamson became Hollywood's teen-material writer of the moment, the WB rolled the dice and signed him up. The gamble paid off: in the two years following *Dawson's Creek's* January 1998 debut, Tinseltown would become Teenseltown as the youth boom mushroomed. "I thought all this would kind of fizzle," Williamson told *New York Times Magazine* in late 1999, "but there is a real audience out there. They don't want to see Bruce Willis or Mel Gibson. They want their own stars like Leo."

UP THE CREEK:
THE 'DAWSON'S' FORMULA

For lack of a better word, it's gonna shock the shit out of people when I sleep with my English teacher.

— Joshua Jackson (Pacey Witter),
in *Entertainment Weekly*, January 1998.

Thanks to modern advances in hype, *Dawson's Creek* was causing a stir even before its broadcast premiere. In an ad campaign that looked more like it was for a $200-million movie than a TV show, the WB pulled out all the stops with artful *Dawson's Creek* billboards in major cities, bus ads, TV spots, and coming-attraction previews in movie theaters. In the fall of 1997, the little town of Wilmington, North Carolina, which stands in for Capeside, Massachusetts, was infiltrated by reporters seeking on-location interviews with the young *Dawson's Creek* cast members. Even though the public had not seen the show yet, the Internet was full of *Dawson's Creek* chatter: a poll on the *UltimateTV* Web site asked potential viewers to grade the show based on the involvement of Kevin Williamson; though they hadn't seen a single episode, 76 percent of respondents gave *Dawson's Creek* an A.

The buzz was instigated by the series' pilot episode, videotapes of which were distributed by the WB's publicity flacks to TV journalists far in advance of the show's debut. The media bit the hook — by November 1997, the *Dawson's Creek* kids had already done cover stories or major interviews with *Entertainment Weekly*, *TV Guide*, YM, and *Seventeen* magazines, *and* the *Access Hollywood* TV show; they did a fashion photo shoot for J. Crew; and they were flown to New York to guest at *Seventeen* magazine's "Hot New Stars" party. "I hope we don't disappoint," James Van Der Beek told the Wilmington

Star-News back in those early days. "We start doing lots of press, lots of photo shoots, and we start to see how many people might watch. It is seductive to think about it." Added his co-star Michelle Williams, "You have to kind of immunize yourself from the hype. That can be real destructive. Ultimately, that's not what matters." But the hype was not all hot air. What the critics responded to, even in the early going, was the intelligence of the characters portrayed in the show. And, not surprisingly, they focused on *Dawson's Creek's* sexual element — although many critics failed to take note that most of the intercourse that takes place is of the verbal variety rather than the bump-and-grind sort.

The universe that Dawson Leery and his friends inhabit was vividly established in the pilot episode. Inside a wooded New England house, Dawson and his platonic best pal Joey are watching Steven Spielberg's childhood fantasy *E.T.* It's a turning point in both their lives; although their choice of movies implies they are still innocents, both are now 15 years old and their respective levels of testosterone and estrogen are rising. Joey, whose mother is dead from cancer and whose father is in jail for marijuana trafficking, has been turning to Dawson for solace and friendship over the course of their 10-year relationship, often sleeping over at his place without an impure thought entering either of their heads. Now that's all about to change. After the movie, Joey says she can't stay over.

"Why?" Dawson wonders aloud. Because she has developed breasts and he's now got genitalia, she says.

"I've always had genitalia," he protests, but Joey reasons, "Now there's more of it."

How does she know this, Dawson asks.

"Long fingers," Joey says.

The other principal players are introduced. Dawson's best friend, Pacey (also 15), is a sarcastic video store clerk who is soon playing Benjamin Braddock to his English teacher's Mrs. Robinson. Meanwhile, adolescent life in Capeside is upended by the arrival of Jen, a 15-year-old New Yorker who's ostensibly there to help her religious grandmother take care of her ill grandfather; what's unspoken (at least at first) is that she's also running away from her dark past in Manhattan, where she was a teen slut. Dawson soon attempts to plant his first smooch on the spicy-hot girl, but when he does, she halts him in mid-pucker.

"Repressing desire can only make it more powerful," Jen says. As the sexually well-heeled woman (she soon reveals she's been sleeping around — since age 12! Better get a blood test, girl!) to Dawson's virginal man-boy, she's street-smart about these things.

The show's frank discussions about sex and masturbation set the stage for a series of complex relationships and happenings that played out over the show's first, abbreviated season (consisting of 13 episodes) and its second (and first full-length) season in 1998–99. Pacey slept with his teacher, then found out she was fooling around with someone else; their affair blew up into a huge scandal and she left town. Joey took up with the pretentious artiste–type Jack McPhee; he told her he was gay and then she ran back to Dawson, Joey's dad got out of jail but he was soon under investigation for drug trafficking again, but before the law could nail him he burned down his tavern (which just happened to be the preferred hangout of Dawson and his gang). Joey's white-trash, trailer-living sister gets impregnated by her black live-in boyfriend; Dawson was equally repulsed by his parents' sexual adventures (mom calls dad "Mr. Man Meat," and Dawson has to knock before entering any room in his house for fear of finding them in the missionary position) and their extramarital affairs. Abby (Monica Keena), the resident bitch, died in a drunken accident; Andie, Pacey's new love interest, went mad; and through it all, both starry-eyed Dawson and tomboy Joey managed to remain virgins — a seemingly major feat — and managed *not* to get together, even though everyone except the two of them knows they're right for each other.

At first glance, *Dawson's Creek* looks like merely a teenage version of *Peyton* (or *Melrose*) *Place*. It owes a nod of appreciation to Archie, the perennial teen of the self-titled comic strip created in 1941 by cartoonist Bob Montana. Like Dawson, Archie was always searching for stability in a world constantly changing around him — Archie has survived World War II, the Cold War, the space race, the sexual revolution, the fall of communism, and so on. And, like Dawson, Archie's life has always been complicated by a love triangle: Betty and Veronica are both attracted to Archie; Jen and Joey vie for Dawson's attention. The model has been used time and again in teen dramas — notably *90210*, which had Brenda and Kelly vying for Dylan's affections. But there's more to *Creek* than a simple formula. The beauty of the show is that there's a character for everyone to identify with. The show's dramatic structure is a complex and appealing web of ambiguous betrayal, twisting irony, and teenage angst; each episode offers a new opportunity to gasp in disbelief, sigh in relief, or groan in disgust. It's a warts-and-all world, as opposed to the air-brushed perfection of the *Beverly Hills, 90210* kids; Dawson Leery wears his awkwardness on his sleeve, and Pacey and the others' faults are in full view, too. More than anything, the show is probably best known for the hip, media-keen intelligence that the characters possess, and which is a standard feature of all of Williamson's work. On the brighter side, Williamson's cross-referencing of pop culture and the show's reality — from Dawson's Spielberg fixation to the episode originally titled *The Breakfast Club* — allows the characters to drop an entertaining pop-culture reference now and then, adding a dash of levity to the show's serious treatment of adolescent turmoil. These references also lend themselves to the sharp, witty dialogue, and to in-jokes like Pacey's declaration that "*Mighty Ducks* was a great flick" (Joshua Jackson, of course, appeared in the film). In all, there were more than 40 movie references in the pilot episode of *Dawson's Creek*.

Therein lies the rub. If there is one knock that the critics have consistently registered with *Dawson's Creek*, it's this: real teens don't talk that way. Williamson and the show's other creators acknowledge this, but they don't apologize for it. "[Williamson's] voice as it translates through teenagers is very intelligent," James Van Der Beek said in a January 1998 *Chicago Tribune* article. "These characters process what they're feeling and verbalize it without rising above it." And co-star Joshua Jackson added in a TV *Guide* article, "We are very elegant teenagers and we have taken a sound beating for that. These kids may speak with the intellect and the language of 30-year-olds, but they still have the emotional core of 15- and 16-year-olds, and that's why (older viewers) are watching the show. And that's why 15-year-olds watch the show as well, because they can relate on a one-to-one basis with what we're doing."

And then there's the sex. Lots of it — in the dialogue, if not in the flesh. In the very first episode, after Jen arrives in town with all her sexy vibes, Pacey turns to Dawson and queries, "So, you think she's a virgin? Wanna nail her?" While it's hardly uncommon for 15-year-olds to have sex on the brain, these kids seldom seem to think about much else, and there is little evidence that they are interested in their school work, sports, politics, jobs, etc.; the focus of life is sex and movies, especially for Dawson, who continually looks to his mentor Spielberg for a moral center amid the sexual chaos surrounding him — Spielberg, Dawson notes, has never had a sex scene in one of his movies. All this semi-trashy talk briefly excited the folks at the Moral Majority, and in July 1999, *Dawson's Creek* was named the worst television program for families by the Parents Television Council, a conservative watchdog group. The council cited the February 1999 episode in which Jack McPhee came out of the closet and said the show "features an almost obsessive focus on premarital sexual activity." But what the conservatives, and even many television critics, overlook is that the show really isn't so much about sex as it is about sexual coming-of-age. And Kevin Williamson deserves credit for giving the teen characters the moral high ground. There is sex in the show, to give it some ratings-grabbing controversy, but in many instances it is the *adults* who are the perpetrators, like Dawson's newscaster mom having an extramarital affair, while Dawson and friends are left to pick up the pieces. "I don't think any of the episodes are about sex," James Van Der Beek told the *Chicago Tribune* in 1998. "But because it is such a huge issue, it pervades the show. I don't think it's any more sexual than any 15-year-old's mind. It's mild compared to that."

Within two months of its premiere, *Dawson's Creek* was the WB's highest-ranking show in the weekly Nielsen ratings; it also helped boost the ratings of *Buffy the Vampire Slayer*, which was rescheduled in the 8 p.m. Tuesday slot, leading into *Creek* and providing a two-hour whammy of midriff-bearing teen programming. Although it hovered around 80 in the Nielsens — which would make it an outright loser if it were airing on one of the four major networks — *Creek* was still considered an incredible success, for it was the number-one show watched by teens in The Demographic — specifically, teen-age girls. Furthermore, media surveys showed that *Creek* had the fourth most affluent viewership among all network television shows. The WB became so confident of *Creek*'s ability to stand on its own legs that, at the beginning of its sophomore season in 1998–99, the show was moved out of its Tuesday night spot with its cushy *Buffy* lead-in and rescheduled on Wednesday night to compete head-to-head with Fox's now menopausal but still popular *Beverly Hills, 90210*. Did Fox feel threatened by this challenge? Probably — it brought *90210*'s original bad-boy Luke Perry back after a long absence and it reportedly paid Laura Leighton, the sexy-naughty girl from *Melrose Place*, $100,000 per episode to guest-star six times on *90210*. "There's only one way to silence the critics: become an established hit instead of what Dawson is now — a flash-in-the-pan sensation," Joshua Jackson told *Entertainment Weekly* in September 1998. To be fair, *Dawson's Creek* at times seemed more like *Melrose Place* during its second season — Dawson's drinking binge, his dad's chasing after a younger woman, etc. — these things did not always seem to fit the mold established during the first season. But after the show managed to cement its place in the television universe, WB officials promised to ease the show back to its less melodramatic roots in the third season. "It will definitely return to a first-season sensibility," WB Executive Vice-President Jordan Levin told *Entertainment Weekly* in July 1999. "Dawson will have something to say instead of the cast reacting to bigger-than-life plots."

ANGST MUSIC

Dawson's Creek might not be quite the same without it: The Song. Who knows, the show might not have become quite the phenomenon that it is. "I Don't Want To Wait," written and performed by Rockport, Massachusetts, native Paula Cole, is an anthem of earnestness that perfectly captures the show's angsty themes. The song was originally released on Cole's 1997 breakthrough album, *This Fire*, which also included her other big alternative-radio hit, "Where Have All the Cowboys Gone?" *This Fire* received seven Grammy Award nominations, of which Cole won one, the Best New Artist award. Cole, who studied music at Berklee College and formerly played in Peter Gabriel's band, also received a lot of media attention for her unshaven armpits, especially when *Entertainment Weekly* magazine ran a photo layout of her and air-brushed out the offending hair.

In April 1999, a collection of sappy alterna-pop tunes that serve as the background music on various *Dawson's Creek* episodes were released as a collection on the CD *Songs From Dawson's Creek*. In addition to Cole's theme song, the CD also includes "Kiss Me" (a song first made popular when it was used in the Freddie Prinze Jr. film *She's All That*) by the Christian band Sixpence None the Richer, a likable group of youngsters with catchy melodic hooks, and who gleefully boast that they've only been playing their instruments for a few years. Also included are several prominent female artists like Sophie B. Hawkins and Heather Nova, and some abhorrent cuts like "Life's a Bitch" by Shooter and "Did You Ever Love Somebody" by Jessica Simpson. Overall, the CD is anything but profound, but it's darn hummable.

SOURCES

"*Dawson's Creek* cited by council." *Associated Press*. July 13, 1999.

Fretts, Bruce. "*90210* Lukes for its old zip, but it's *Creek's* new trio who are really making a splash." *Entertainment Weekly*. December 4, 1998.

Goodale, Gloria. "Veteran TV producer still unstoppable." *The Christian Science Monitor*. February 12, 1999.

Hirschberg, Lynn. "Desperate to seem 16." *New York Times Magazine*. September 5, 1999.

Houpt, Simon. "Heartthrob High." *TV Guide*. January 30, 1998.

Jacobs, A. J. "Staking a claim." *Entertainment Weekly*. March 6, 1998.

Kloer, Phil. "The *Creek* is rising; on the set with Dawson and friends as their popularity soars among teenagers in Atlanta and nationally." *Atlanta Constitution*. October 7, 1998

Nashawaty, Chris. "Teen steam; sparked by a sexy new brat pack, a youthquake is blowing the lid off Hollywood." *Entertainment Weekly*.November 14, 1997.

Pennington, Gail. "And one to grow on; the scaremeister who brought us *Scream* has turned his attention to a new TV show about Teenagers." *St. Louis Post-Dispatch*. January 20, 1998.

Roberts, Lee. "Everyone's watching; *Dawson's Creek*." *Sunday Star-News* (Wilmington, NC). November 2, 1997.

Shaw, Jessica. "News & notes; the hills are alive; with an eighth set, can Fox's melodramatic chestnut stay fresh?" *Entertainment Weekly*. February 7, 1997.

Snierson, Dan. "The sophomore; kept afloat by a sea of teen fans, *Dawson's Creek* dives into its second season — and tries to swim with the big fish of *Beverly Hills, 90210*." *Entertainment Weekly*. September 11, 1998.

Tucker, Ken. "Five Alive; After five years of earnest angsting and life-lesson learning, those Salinger siblings are still going strong." *Entertainment Weekly*. April 30, 1999.

EPISODE GUIDE

Starring: James Van Der Beek as Dawson Leery

Katie Holmes as Josephine "Joey" Potter

Joshua Jackson as Pacey Witter

Michelle Williams as Jen Lindley

Mary-Margaret Humes as Gale Leery

John Wesley Shipp as Mitchell Leery

Mary Beth Peil as Evelyn "Grams" Ryan

Nina Repeta as Bessie Potter

Meredith Monroe as Andie McPhee

Kerr Smith as Jack McPhee

Monica Keena as Abby Morgan

100 — PILOT
(FORMERLY EMOTIONS IN MOTION)*

Written by Kevin Williamson
Directed by Steve Miner
Originally aired January 20, 1998

Guest starring: Leann Hunley (Tamara Jacobs), Mitchell Laurance (Benjamin Gold), Ted King (Bob Collinsworth), Obi Ndefo (Bodie)

The first episode of *Dawson's Creek* crackles with adolescent danger. Dawson Leery and Joey Potter are at a crossroads, where a lifelong friendship is suddenly thrown into strange new pubescent territory. Dawson's best friend, the self-esteem-challenged Pacey, is about to fall headlong into the stormy world of illicit adult romance with his teacher. Jennifer Lindley, a luscious blonde from New York, has just landed at Capeside, batting her eyelashes and pouting her lips. She's a mysterious outsider whose wide eyes may have seen enough to hurry half the teenage male population into seriously advanced rites of passage. Even Dawson's parents, who roll around on the kitchen table as if the postman had rung twice, are on the verge of devastating revelations about the source of their accelerated marital lust.

Williamson has each of his characters riding the rim of instabilities, and in perfect shorthand he skips long establishing material and throws us smack in the middle of a

*Williamson originally used movie titles as the titles of the episodes in the first season, but when he ran into copyright problems he had to retitle them.

world on the brink of breathtaking change. As much as the characters arrive fully drawn, Williamson imbues his first episode with a technique that is familiar to fans of *Scream*: abundant referentiality. The world of Capeside is familiar in the way that *Beverly Hills, 90210* is — this is *Archie*. With a little switch of hair color, Dawson is Archie, Joey is Betty, Pacey is Reggie, and Jen is Veronica. However, unlike the comic–book world of *Archie*, where teenagers remain snug in their sophomore year for decades, the kids of *Dawson's Creek* confront these types, bringing them back to a real world. What if Reggie really did step over the line sexually? What if Archie and Betty were confronted by the uncomfortable incestuous dimension of romantic pairings in Riverdale? What if in her ambition to appear worldly, Veronica fell to the temptations of an underworld? And what if the oddly bad-tempered adults of Riverdale became passionate, lustful, and dishonest?

The traumatic changes Williamson sets up are powerful because he has created believable characters to whom viewers can relate, but he has also dropped a bomb in middle America's institution of memory. This time, when Veronica checks out Betty's beachwear it's not because they are wearing the same thing, it's to tell her that she has "nice breasts." The two contradictory levels that Williamson builds on here — that these are more like teenagers than Archie and his gang, but also more like comic–book characters — puts another fascinating and striking gap in the first episode. Who isn't asking, by the time the hour's up: Do teenagers really talk like that? The sophisticated, analytical dialogue will even split cast and creators into two camps: the teenage stars will say this is teenage verité, and Williamson will call it parody.

Place is also introduced as an emotional setting. The glittery sunlit river is both the outer world's way in and a constant reminder that there is a journey yet to be made *out* of Capeside. The bustling hallway of the high school, the cliqued-off cafeteria, and the theater of the classroom will all become treacherous little settings as the season unfolds. Then there's the ladder up to Dawson's bedroom, which transforms the teenager's entire house into a tree that supports his childhood clubhouse. We first witness Joey using it with tomboyish aplomb, but when she overhears Dawson and Jen in intimate conversation, is this youthful contraption about to undergo irreversible change? Williamson will focus on this ladder over and over again, allowing it to oscillate between being an innocent piece of childhood apparatus and a Shakespearean trellis up, which star-crossed lovers climb and where terrible misunderstandings gather.

101 — DANCE
(FORMERLY DIRTY DANCING)

Written by Kevin Williamson
Directed by Steve Miner
Originally aired January 27, 1998

Guest starring: Scott Foley (Cliff Elliott), Leann Hunley (Tamara Jacobs), Mitchell Laurance (Benjamin Gold), Obi Ndefo (Bodie)

If the first episode is projected against *Archie*, the second is screen-in-screen, introducing Williamson's other major theme. One of the ways the kids break type is to cast new ones: at times, quite literally. Dawson, the young aspiring filmmaker, will fulfil many of Williamson's autobiographical points. The camera here isn't just a recording device or a creative tool, it's a mirror that will alter relationships. The horror film becomes a teenage game of truth or dare: Joey refuses to kiss Pacey and is replaced by Jen as Dawson's star. In a competing scenario, football jock Cliff (a natural Moose) has managed to woo Jen over to his set, displacing Dawson, who is confused as to whether it is his creative life or his romantic life that is falling flat.

Jen is the wild card, having intimated to Dawson that her life in New York was regrettably fast, and her intentions are baffling and exotic to the relatively unworldly Capeside Film Boy. When she gravitates toward Cliff/Moose, the arrogant Dawson is triggered: I'm the complex, talented one, why him? (It's interesting to note that despite Dawson's constant mockery of Cliff's movie, *Helmets of Glory*, Van Der Beek would end up starring in a very similar film, *Varsity Blues*.) He is, of course, mistaking the character of Jen for that of Joey, who knows Dawson and, more importantly, knows how Dawson likes to be treated. Dawson is a fairly self-serving character who will frequently mistake his vanity for sensitivity. He cannot see that Jen, who has been manipulated by males in the past, has chosen the director whom she can direct. This leads to a classic Dawson Leery outburst when he loutishly tries to cut in during a slow dance between Jen and Cliff. When the sensitive artist bursts into the arena of action, look out: he's in world of his own.

Joey, on the other hand, is the show's voyeur. In the first episode, she overhears Dawson and Jen talking. In this episode she hears Dawson's mother talking to the man with whom she's having an affair. The doubling of events is one of Williamson's trademarks, as he makes repetition part of how things become significant. Joey perceives an infidelity she cannot identify in the innocent conversation between Jen and Dawson. This infidelity is confirmed loud and clear when she overhears Dawson's mother involved in a much less innocent

James at the Emmy Awards.

conversation with a strange man. Joey steps in on this second situation and stops Mrs. Leery dead in her tracks to confront her. There is no question that Mrs. Leery is wrong in her adultery, but the uncomfortable feeling here is that she is also being punished for her son's perceived romantic crimes. Because the emotional relationships of these teenagers are changing wildly and fast, they are often made catastrophic through misidentification.

When Dawson and Joey leave the dance together, reverting as they will often do to the outmoded intimacy of pals, they spot Jen standing on the dock. This time, rather than give her feelings voice, Joey steps aside and releases Dawson to Jen. It is, after all, inevitable, and it allows Joey to escape the possibility that she was never the romantic lead to begin with. Joey seems to find a sad comfort in being the betrayed and she has cast herself this way, not by seizing any role, but by observing others. One of the ways Joey's see-and-not-be-seen character *does* become a romantic subject is the short-lived fantasy identity she concocts for herself to get a rich outsider's attention in the next episode. Not only is she taking an emotional holiday, she ceases to exist as Joey Potter. Her strategy is not as wrong-headed as it sounds, though. There are no guarantees that acting on your feelings is its own reward. Witness Dawson's embarrassing debacle at the dance. He may have Jen's attention now, but can he keep it? Does he even know where these feelings come from?

The real cautionary tale is developing between Pacey and Ms. Jacobs. Pacey has taken his teacher's reckless flirtations at face value. To Pacey the look is hard romantic currency and he aggressively tries to cash it in. Having ham-handedly interfered on a date his teacher is having at the movies, Pacey ignores everything but the implied attraction. That the relationship is a foreshadowed disaster eludes him, and he persists. One of the interesting features of *Dawson's Creek* is the overwhelming force of passions that are frequently destructive, and when Tamara submits, the roles of mentor and student are turned upside down. If there's one thing these kids are aware of, it's that they all sit at the wellspring of powerful feelings.

102 — KISS
(FORMERLY A PRELUDE TO A KISS)

Written by Rob Thomas
Directed by Michael Uno
Originally aired February 3, 1998

Guest starring: Ian Bohen (Anderson Crawford), Scott Foley (Cliff Elliott), Leann Hunley (Tamara Jacobs), Mitchell Laurance (Benjamin Gold), Obi Ndefo (Bodie)

In this episode the disasters brewing are not averted; instead they're given the full *Dawson's Creek* treatment. The lessons that seemed to be tidily taught to otherwise responsible intelligent teenagers are recklessly unlearned in order to make way for the wilder experience of finding things out for yourself. The "lesson" is played out quite literally in Pacey's case. It seems the young cut-up is failing to perform academically and is called in after class by Tamara. In a pretty sexy bit of dialogue, they work out a deal wherein the teacher is going to give the student experience in exchange for some right answers. It's a very hot little set piece that distinguishes *Dawson's Creek* as a show for teenagers that doesn't pull back on its adult themes. When Pacey surprises Tamara by coming up with the right answers, the teacher decides to call his bluff and becomes aggressive and coarse toward the teenager, ordering him to strip. When Pacey folds, revealing his virginity, Tamara looks shocked and attempts to cut him loose. The interesting turn here is that despite Pacey's virginity, it is Tamara who is confronted by her inexperience; she is getting in over her head. It is Pacey's ability to be direct — emotionally and psychologically — that will lead this relationship, not the older woman's knowledge. These are more than references to *The Graduate* and *The Summer of '42* — they are Capeside re-writes, and a signal to the viewer. Like Ibsen's law — which states that if a gun appears in the first act it'll go off by the end of the play — if a film where an older woman takes the virginity of a young boy is referenced in the first episode, it's no bluff. The sparks will fly.

While Joey is working through her *Mystic Pizza* fantasy with Yacht Boy, Dawson is busy trying to script his first kiss with Jen. In Dawson's inimitable style, he packs the moment with more of his own self-serving commentary than any real romance, and the scene is written in a patented Williamson high concept. Dawson has actually set up a video camera to tape their first kiss! For Dawson, the sentimental idealist, whose emotions are truest when he's watching Frank Capra films for the fifteenth time, his first kiss won't even be real until he has a chance to watch it played back. This is perfectly presented when Dawson resolves a technical problem on his rival Cliff's film set. Dawson improvises a tracking shot with the use of wheelchair, giving an emblematic warning that Dawson's ingenuity has the capacity to cripple him. There are some sinister dimensions to Dawson's struggle to achieve meaningful relationships, and in the complex atmosphere of Capeside the means quickly contaminate the ends. If as Dawson attempts to woo Jen for his camera he is committing a crime of dispassion, then he need only look a little deeper in the woods, for there is the real thing: the hot-for-teacher Pacey and the "touched for the very first time" Tamara are showing the woodland creatures how it is really done. Though Jen and Dawson can't see who the couple are, the camera at least knows a real love scene when it sees it, and the stand-ins for Dawson's first kiss are unwittingly ready for their close-up.

103 — DISCOVERY
(FORMERLY CARNAL KNOWLEDGE)

Written by Jon Harmon Feldman
Directed by Steve Miner
Originally aired February 10, 1998

Guest starring: Leann Hunley (Tamara Jacobs), Mitchell Laurance (Benjamin Gold), Ric Reitz (Bob Collinsworth)

Now that enough potential disasters have been set in motion, it's time to let a couple hit the fan. Pacey is discovered on videotape as the woodland lover and confesses to Dawson. Dawson sees his own mother kissing her co-anchor, and she becomes the wife who, between the accusing innuendoes of Dawson and Joey, has a fair collection of scarlet letters to hide from her husband. But if this storyline is about the foibles of adults and the danger of protracted adolescence, it's also about the inflammable superiority of children when confronted by their parents as real, flawed human beings. The haughty look on Dawson's face and his condemnatory tone as he lords morally and falsely potent in his parents' home is painful to watch. The sympathy does not lie with him, though he seems to assume it should, and the guilt-stricken fear of his mother and the odd puppy love her husband feels for her seem far more human than Dawson's moon-faced hostility and indignation. It is at times difficult to like Dawson: the viewer is challenged time and time again to be understanding toward a character in ways he himself seems incapable of doing. Dawson inflates himself with the scandal, and somewhat grotesquely launches a crusade for honesty and fidelity. He revels in his superiority, soliciting Joey as his acolyte, only to be snagged on the fact that Joey had been keeping the secret of his mother's affair from him all along. Dawson is far from understanding of the complicated position Joey has been in and he abandons her in disgust to head for higher ground.

Jen is initially impressed by Dawson's mission to live in a world of full disclosure and she decides, in this spirit, to tell Dawson about the excesses of her past. Well, Dawson, be careful what you ask for. As Dawson responds to Jen's confession in a callous and judgmental fashion, it's obvious that our "hero" is in great danger of living a life he himself hasn't examined. The cloud around him — a cloud of arrogance and superiority — has made him blind to the emotional lives of others, and he projects this failure of his own onto what he perceives are flaws in others. The theme of this episode is central to the entire season: the alienation of Dawson. What Williamson does here is throw the challenge back to us by ultimately alienating his protagonist from the audience's sympathy. Do we like Dawson? If we do, it's not because he impresses us with his goodness. We are forced to respect the journey in spite of the person taking it. We want the same respect. We are all trying, and if we can be patient with Dawson, then we too are learning an important piece in our own journey.

104 — HURRICANE
(FORMERLY BLOWN AWAY)

Written by Kevin Williamson and Dana Baratta
Directed by Lou Antonio
Originally aired February 12, 1998

Guest starring: Leann Hunley (Tamara Jacobs),
Ric Reitz (Bob Collinsworth), Dylan Neal (Deputy Doug Witter),
Obi Ndefo (Bodie)

As Hurricane Chris gathers strength, so does the first season of *Dawson's Creek* and the various plotlines all reach critical mass under some pretty heavy weather. This is a *tour de force* episode, where Williamson unites time, place, and action in a single thunderclap, bruising his cast in an atmosphere as emotionally frightening as a Greek tragedy. The wind and rain whip Mrs. Leery around the yard as she trails after her stony husband like a guilty thing surprised. In a series of lightning flashes, Dawson has not only confronted his mother, he has practically branded her with a scarlet letter, and she is forced to throw herself at the mercy of her husband. Dawson is now quivering with righteous indignation, and his behavior seems almost manic, almost pathological against the backdrop of the hurricane. There is a real sense of danger in these scenes, that unforeseen forces are being unleashed by the various high betrayals and low passions of the characters. Mr. Leery becomes a different person: previously a playful and oblivious husband, he turns into a dangerous cipher of wrath, baiting his adulterous wife with a sentimental tone, then coldly snapping her hopes to bits.

This scene, played out in the rain-lashed family car parked in the driveway, intensifies the adult dimension of the emotions that Dawson has degraded with his high-flown principles. Mitch's pain is profound and frightening. Gale, who had been a woman leading a double life, collapses, making her an abject figure. Of all the characters huddling in the storm, she is the one who seems to be the hurricane's plaything. The emotions are drawn so large and dangerous in these scenes that they recall the atmosphere of a Brontë novel, with deadly, immovable passions and human drama touching on madness. As the storm passes, the husband and wife finally allow each other's company; however, this is more exhaustion than reconciliation and there is no question that they have changed. Most television shows are about resolving complications in order to restore balance. One of the interesting things about Williamson's characters is that the balance is uncovered to be its own unresolved complication. There is no question of restoration, and characters are forced to experiment with new balances.

While this drama is playing out in the Leery household, Pacey and Tamara are playing out a comic version of these dangerous adult themes. During a harmless board game, Pacey observes Tamara flirting with his brother, Deputy Doug. Pacey slyly uses his own running gag that his brother is gay to throw Tamara off the trail. The deception is humorous and formulated by an adolescent who feels at the margins of a grown-up exchange due to his age. When his ruse is discovered, Doug pulls his handgun on Pacey, forcing him to tell the truth. The gun, an adult symbol, is suddenly a toy. Tamara would be wise to take note of the transformation — her own boy-toy might soon himself become a smoking gun.

The concluding scenes of this episode are, in keeping with its classical atmosphere, drenched in a post-cathartic glow. The storm has changed them all, and no one can say for certain if this is for the better, or if they have all become lesser people. For now, they cope with exhaustion by acting out safe regression. Joey and Dawson are suddenly forgetful of all the adult themes, fatigued by them and they retreat to an age before the world went mad. They hide in the closet — literally closeting their feelings for each other — and act out a scene from *Jaws*, reliving a time when the most dangerous thing in their lives was a mechanical shark named Bruce.

105 — BABY
(FORMERLY LOOK WHO'S TALKING)

Written by Jon Harmon Feldman
Directed by Steve Miner
Originally aired February 24, 1998

Guest Starring: Leann Hunley (Tamara Jacobs),
Obi Ndefo (Bodie), Ed Brady (Gramps Ryan)

Tamara's little pistol now becomes, officially, the smoking gun. Pacey and Tamara's illicit affair is spread by a rumor whose source is an overheard conversation between Dawson and Pacey. At first blush it would appear to be the product of the teenager bragging on a conquest; however, it is more of a confession coerced by Dawson. This confusion will be a defining point for the compelling character of Pacey, whose reckless swaggering may be a dimension of his as yet unrealized integrity and intelligence. (Dawson, on the other hand, acts as if he was the most fastidiously principled kid in Capeside, while bluntly missing the point left and right.) It's Pacey's loose and reckless behavior that opens him up to locating exactly where the head sits on the nail, and in due course it's Pacey who will hit it precisely. Tamara is brought before an inquiring body to answer for her alleged affair. She may resent the source of these allegations, but she is faced with the fact that she has been playing in a teenage world and must now pay for her dalliance in an adult one. Astonishingly, Pacey recognizes the stakes here and he interrupts the inquiry by telling the board he has made the entire thing up. In this one act Pacey becomes a complex and appealing person. He is willing to obey type and to fall in line with his own history of attention seeking in order to protect a person he has deep feelings for. His act is remarkable in that it gives him no advantage whatsoever and is an entirely selfless act through which he loses face and the woman he clearly loves. In this episode, Pacey gets at something Dawson misses entirely — that you are not merely how you are perceived by others. While Dawson watches the movie screen for a place to grow up, Pacey is aware that the audience leaves. One of the cautions implicit in *Dawson's Creek*, however, is that when one character appears to be the correction of Dawson, there is no insurance against that character applying it to a fault. When he stands before Tamara afterward, the swagger that he had so nobly avoided comes out: he's here to claim his reward. Wrong. Tamara not only refuses to be the prize, she's leaving Capeside altogether. As Pacey wanders away dejected, his only reward is to be alone with the powerful feelings he took such pains to honor. The inner life of Pacey Whitter has now been tapped and will become the show's most fascinating resource.

The other theme developing is Jen's exile from the fast lane to her Grams' restrictive Christian guardianship. Grams is another type who is cast poorly at first. She appears to be controlling and pious, with very little to warm her; she's even given the unforgivable trait of apparent racism. Jen's character, on the other hand, is an intelligent and liberal young woman.

The consequences of her excesses are minimized as they appear merely to be an inevitable phase. These two types are in such characteristic opposition that ascribing qualities is almost automatic: Jen is good, Grams is bad. The first destabilizing of this false opposition occurs when Grams must act as midwife at the birth of a mixed-race baby. It is common knowledge that she disapproves of families of mixed race, so she is forced to come to the pregnant woman's aid under a great deal of protest from both mother-to-be and her own granddaughter. However, it becomes apparent throughout the course of the birth that Grams *isn't* racist, but concerned about exposing the child to the prejudices of the world it will be born into: prejudicial minds ironically like those that have abused her with knee-jerk assumptions about the type of woman she is. While we now seem to understand her lack of confidence in people, it is something so engendered in her religiousness that it contradicts, to some extent, her faith. This is perhaps the fault she exhibits, and it is not easy for Jen to reassess her Grams. This young woman's prejudice involves not seeing Grams as a complex woman. Both of these characters are again misapplied correctives to each other, who will have to accept the difficult possibility that they bear a powerful resemblance to one another.

(FORMERLY THE BREAKFAST CLUB)

Written by Mike White
Directed by Al Arkush
Originally aired March 3, 1998

Guest starring: Helen Baldwin (Mrs. Tingle), Barry Bell (coach),
Mati Moralego (Grant Bodine)

Like the hurricane episode, "Detention" is one built around an occasion. It seems that for one reason or another, all our fab kids have suffered from little bouts of delinquency, landing them in a dreaded Saturday detention. If the storm was broadly referencing atmospheres both moor and heath, then the detention is a little more specific: welcome to *The Breakfast Club*. These are the dog days of adolescence, when simple debts are paid for acting out in the playground. Pacey has taunted Dawson with the childhood name "Oompa loompa" and gets his nose bashed for the pleasure. In fact, one of the tying themes here is how embar-rassments of that proportion make teenage life seem suddenly an unbearable comedy. Picture Pacey: the poor fellow's just been identified as the source of the rumor that he slept with a teacher. Now he's stumbling into Saturday detention with a nose like Krusty. Add to that the reason he's there in the first place: in a state of arousal the lad slipped off from the gym to, uh, . . . ahem . . . to relieve himself, only to be discovered and sent — slapping a hairy palm to his forehead — to the detention hall. To survive these embarrassments our young friend is going to need a fairly deep well of self-esteem.

An interesting feature of the *Breakfast Club* reference is that it is identified by the kids themselves: this isn't merely a situation derived from a movie, this is an occasion that existed *before* the movie. This is the detention from which the film derived, not the other way around. Recognizing the connection, the kids act out the drama accordingly, playing its game of Truth or Dare in a way that reveals the postmodern to be less a strategy for reading than an obvious feature of teenage life in the nineties. And in keeping with the film, this is a day to test the truth. Kisses are dared under watchful looks and games of one-on-one sort out the male order. For all its drama, much of this is playful experimentation. When Joey gives Pacey a soulful kiss, the kids are not discovering a latent romance between the two; instead, they are in the presence of an entirely new toy: eroticism. And with this explosive toy they are discovering that emotional meaningfulness is not a simple flowing forth of unstoppered desire. It is a complicated minefield that requires a certain responsibility: whom they kiss will matter as much as whom they secretly *want* to kiss. The heavy lessons of erotica, however, are only a momentary diversion before they bounce off into a new game. It's time to pull down our pants, sit on the photocopier, and play Guess My Butt. There are a number of ways to perpetuate the game of sizing each other up without actually having to do anything about it. If responsibility and truth-testing are the serious notes of this episode, its other equally important part is that irresponsibility is a necessary joy. Without it, the dare might destroy you, and the truth might just claim more than it really owns.

107 — BOYFRIEND
(FORMERLY ESCAPE FROM NEW YORK)

Written by Jon Harmon Feldman and Dana Baratta
Directed by Charles Rosin and Karen Rosin
Originally aired March 10, 1998

Guest starring: Eion Bailey (Billy Konrad), Scott Foley (Cliff Elliott), Jeremy Moore (Tyler)

Dawson Leery is in many ways an unlikely heartthrob figure. Unlike say, *90210*'s Dylan, Dawson is neither mad nor bad. And he is definitely not dangerous to know. He's self-absorbed and self-righteous. For all his supposed analytical prowess, he is more often than not moralistic and insensitive. As an artist, Dawson Leery has a hopelessly conservative imagination. On the Byron scale Dawson Leery is as pale a shade of hunk as there ever was. Even Pacey cuts a dashing figure beside the nebbish loverboy. In a word, Dawson, along with all the other characteristics that keep us from ever fully sympathizing with him, is just not cool. So when a leatherclad bit of ex-boyfriend named Billy shows up in Capeside to claim Dawson's Jen, his already devalued stock takes a nose dive. It is this crisis that gives the viewer indirect access to feeling for Dawson, as the indomitable cool of Billy appears like a mythic figure, a Michael Fury, representing a world utterly unlike Capeside. Dawson is forced to fall back on his own rocky record and take stock of exactly who he is.

The central character here is Jen. On either side of her are men who represent to her almost entirely opposite worlds. Billy is bad, Dawson is good. Her choice isn't clear to her and her attractions are confused by these two poles, forcing Jen to make the feminist choice; that is, a life without men. The decision she

THE YEY DON'T WANNA WAIT

Michelle Williams and James Van Der Beek.

comes to is surprisingly harmonious with the restrictions Grams would impose on her wild granddaughter. One set of opposites, in Dawson and Billy, is cemented on either side of Jen, and through her they become the same: men who want all her attention. This gives rise to another set of opposites collapsing: that of the elderly Christian and the young recovering rebel. Jen, like Pacey, has an independent personality, thereby forcing people around her to look within and examine themselves. Dawson, on the other hand, has a habit of seeking himself in others, adding confusion to indecision. Joey, for instance, finds herself dissolving in Dawson's attention. Is she his love interest or just his most familiar friend? Or some of both, and more of one, depending on who's on the fellow's dance card? Enough. Joey also abandons the strange male animal and plunges herself in studies to the point where Pacey grows alarmed at her shrinking world. He decides the best thing would be to take her to a party so that she can let loose a bit. Just as the Truth or Dare game revealed a potent and not always romantic device in the kiss, the teenage ritual of drunken makeout sessions at house parties proves to be an emotional nightmare in the making. Joey, of course, ends up being nearly assaulted by an available Mr. Wrong, only to be rescued by Dawson, the Dudley Do-Right on the stairs. Well, is this the heroic narrative that will reveal true hearts to one and all? Not likely: when the Prince kisses Sleeping Beauty, she doesn't quite awake from her deadly sleep, because, unfortunately, she's had a few. The Prince is impressed, but what with the booze on her breath, who can tell? Again Dawson is confused by the blurring of Jen into Joey, so he runs off to find the former, almost as if to confirm that his girls are two different people. And different they are. Dawson hits the wall of the real Jen's sober decision to be independent, and the Prince finds himself cast in with all the other frogs who have been kissed by beautiful women.

108 — ROAD TRIP
(FORMERLY IN THE COMPANY OF MEN)

Written by Rob Thomas
Directed by Steve Robman
Originally aired March 17, 1998

Guest starring: Eion Bailey (Billy Konrad),
Eric Balfour (Warren Goering), Jeremy Moore (Tyler)

This episode is a midsummer night's dream of deception, misdirected affection, and pretense. The midnight is signaled by the moon: in one of several references to *American Graffiti*, Pacey squeezes his bare butt out a car window, to taunt some toughs. How did the boys — Pacey, Dawson, and Billy — become wild in Providence? Well, Billy managed to wiggle his way into Jen's bed back at Capeside, only to be banished by Grams, who turfs him so far out of the house he just doesn't seem to want to stop running. But just 'cause our Bad Boy is running doesn't mean he can't keep playing. So he dangles his flight in front of Pacey and Dawson in the form of a bonding episode, tempting them with the wild regions that lie beyond Capeside and beyond their experience.

While the boys are doing a feasibility study for Toad's wild ride, Joey enacts her own little drama of deceit. It seems Warren Goering, a friendly chap really, gives Joey a ride to school. But it's not just any old ride, it's a bit of a trip through a funhouse. The next thing she knows, the helpful Warren has helped himself to bragging rights on a night of passion with his little brown-eyed hitch-hiker. Except (like it even needs to be said) Joey, the girl voted "Least Likely To Give It Away For Anyone Soon," is still a demure virgin.

Well, almost. Maybe not quite demure. In fact, the

rumor inspires her to a hot round of hot air and before long, she has all of Capeside believing that she's not only sleeping with guys to get a ride to school, but, this particular fellow has got her pregnant! However, something at the center of the rumors (perhaps the secret source of the original rumor itself) deflates everything. Literally. Warren, apparently, was never up to the task in the first place.

If the hormone wagons of Capeside have circled around a young man's budding inadequacy, in Providence the wily Billy-boy is sowing the seed that may lead to Dawson starting to, well, sow seeds. By tempting him with strange women in a strange world, Billy hopes Dawson will forget about Jen and, maybe, Jen will forget about him. As the night progresses, the dream flirt turns out to have feet of clay and our boys, with wild stars still glittering in the heads, head home.

As the film *Clueless* was to Jane Austen's *Emma*, this episode is to Shakespeare's *Midsummer Night's Dream*. Both pieces manage to ring the timeless themes without ever leaving the era in which they are depicted. As Joey and Dawson fall asleep on Dawson's bed, too tired to share their adventures, they conjure the spellbound dreamers in Shakespeare's weird and wonderful classic.

109 — DOUBLE DATE
(FORMERLY MODERN ROMANCE)

Written by Jon Harmon Feldman
Directed by David Semel
Originally aired April 24, 1998

Guest starring: Scott Foley (Cliff Elliott),
Meghan Perry (Mary Beth)

One of the obvious problems with shows about teenage romance is the limited pairings that are available within the cast. A kind of dreariness sinks in as viewers begin to grow less credulous with each attempt to make the fortieth version of the same infidelity seem fresh. But, the funny thing is, that's exactly what happens. The world isn't populated by the love children of Mr. and Mrs. Right. Nope, we are the offspring of Mr. Right and Mrs. Right's best friend. Love doesn't become destiny across distant lands, it's only destiny if it places us side by side. And if it's destiny that places us together, then it's also destiny that ensures that when we fall out of love, it's because we were meant to fall in love with the roommate. The plot limitations of a show like *90210* are also ours. *90210* doesn't know it, but the creators of *Dawson's Creek* do, and in this episode, we have left the world of the Shakespearean dream and have been thrust into a harsher Sophoclean arena where our kids are the playthings of the gods. Specifically, they are Pacey and Joey's remedial snails in science class.

Pacey and Joey have to get a pair of snails to mate in order for them to get badly needed extra credit. These are our gods, of course, the Fates who have placed potential lovers side by side in a little experiment. What drives the fates to bring love into the world? Depends. Pacey needs to bring his mark up from a 32 (this particular god is neglectful). Joey wants to bring hers up from a 98 (this god has been paying so much attention to things she's a little off her rocker). The device is used to great effect, underlying the way that close proximity and arbitrary events will attempt to determine the course of romance.

The lab experiment begins. Dawson still can't accept the loss of Jen, who is now dating someone else and leaving him out in the cold. What he needs to get close to her is not to do what her new date is doing, but what Jen herself is doing, and, importantly to do this is at the same time and the same place. Solution: the double date. Make the environment symmetrical. Back at the remedial Lab, Pacey our neglectful god has skipped this lesson and he decides to scoop up a pretty-looking snail and toss it in the tank to sexy up the atmosphere. Problem is, his casual and arbitrary act — the introduction of a hot-looking single into the mix — goes in and literally devours the slimy little paramours.

Cut to the double-date experiment at the carnival. A little natural swapping has occurred and Dawson and Jen are together for the time being, carried aloft by a huge Ferris wheel. Well, quicker than you can say "Pacey, you moron!" the Ferris wheel, a handy sign of fortune in play, comes to a screeching halt. Has destiny conspired with Dawson's desires? Does Jen have any hope of resisting such impressive cosmic machinery? Short answer: yes. There's more to life than slime trails in the terrarium and Jen trumps the whole experiment with her independence: No to Dawson. No to the stars. No to the gods. And no to the snails.

One of the interesting psychological motifs of this episode is the waffling commitment. Dawson has invested elaborate designs to make Jen's decision inevitable, overlooking the simple fact of her independent desire. He is, perhaps, projecting onto the world his own indecisiveness. When Pacey's thrown, like his snails, into close proximity to Joey, he, of course, feels the compulsion to give her a kiss. When he asks for Dawson's approval (and gets a series of mixed messages from him) and then does what feels natural in the moment, Dawson is struck between the eyes by feelings he had not allowed. Dawson never wanted Pacey to kiss Joey. They kiss, or at least nearly do, pulling back, giving arbitrary circumstances their only real chance to determine a course for romance. The missing factor had been the knowledge of strong feelings. And here the episode hangs, a host of possibilities waiting to be shown. Who does Dawson want to be with? He had better hurry, because fate will only repeat itself so many times.

110 — THE SCARE
(FORMERLY FRIDAY THE 13TH)

Written by Mike White
Directed by Rodman Flender
Originally aired May 5, 1998

Guest starring: Scott Foley (Cliff Elliott),
Jennifer McComb (Ursula), Mitchell Laurance (Benjamin Gold),
Justin Smith (Eddie)

Here it comes. Definitely one of the scariest hours ever put on television. One of the formulas unique to the drama on *Dawson's Creek* is to have elements reinforce each other in direct and powerful ways. A show like *Party of Five*, for instance, will use the fugue construction of ensemble storylines to counterpoint emotions. One storyline will have a tragic betrayal and the next a joyful new beginning, creating a scope that contains pockets of difference. It is effective and each pocket against the other conveys an overall sense of searching characters. *Dawson's Creek* is constructed in a much bolder fashion. If it's raining on one side of town, it's raining a little harder on the other end. This is often apparent in the high-concept episodes, where the *Dawson's Creek* creators are not afraid to have a little fun letting a conceit control the characters. This also allows for some unrelenting intensity you might not have if you always played the drama off supple character situations. Remember the mighty storm? Not the subtlest backdrop to revelations of infidelity, but it sure was an emotionally breathtaking way to play it.

This particular episode takes place on Friday the thirteenth, so we know right off the bat that all hell's going to break loose. (Did anybody go to see the film *Scream* expecting to read subtitles?) So let's start stuffing fake snakes in handbags and ghoulish heads in lockers, because it's all about setting the mood now. The interesting challenge in such an all-encompassing theme is how to move the romantic tangles along in a tightly wound horror plot. The device — used correctly — mirrors the logic of a horror film: who's gonna get it and who's doing it? Good questions to ask in either a *Scream* or a *Creek* scenario.

At first it appears that Jen is being ignored in a series of practical jokes, situating her clearly outside the group. Question number one: is she the one who's really going to get it? Number two: who's going to do it to her? And sure enough, the one prank that seems genuinely threatening, a frightening crank call, has Jen asking herself whether Dawson was leaving her out of his nightmare only to reserve her spot center stage for a less comfortable game? Meanwhile, the hapless Cliff is having trouble keeping Jen's attention, so he defers to the supposed master of ceremonies, Dawson, who sends him away to concoct his own devilishness. The caller slowly becomes anybody's guess and, in fact, the whole game is being breached left and right by very real dangers. A serial killer is afoot. Somewhere out there in the night is a sick predator who might, at any moment, raise the stakes in Dawson's fun to terrible heights.

And now Pacey (the god who likes attractive and deadly snails) has introduced an entirely new and unknown character into this episode's "terrorium." Outside a convenience store, a damsel is in distress and she approaches Pacey, who is waiting for the others in a car. She is seeking protection from her violent boyfriend, Eddie. Big mistake. Once they have her back at the house to resume their scary parlor games, the Capeside players realize they have picked up a girl with a decidedly dangerous edge. She and the creepy Eddie are of a piece and pretty soon he's snatching at everybody through broken glass. The contrasts used in this episode to create fear are very effective. Dawson's games have a limited scare factor. They are of the cat-bursting-through-a-window variety and are the cheap thrill found in any devised horror film, but they aren't the only horror film in town. At mid-level on the scare meter is the whole *Scream* franchise that cuts through the group like a thin garrote in the form of an unidentified phone call. Not knowing who's doing it is enough to make Dawson's tactics seem pedestrian. The horror all begins to go up by notches. What's worse than not knowing who's playing the game? Well, maybe innocently inviting someone in who changes the rules to a much darker code. When Ursula and Eddie start releasing their violent energy on our gang, the group is confronted with all that they keep at bay, namely, real anger, real danger, and real destruction.

These plots are brought to resolutions that conform in a satisfying way with their horror film roots. Eddie the monster is stopped by Joey the virgin, driven out by that power invested in virgins in all proper horror film endings. Is that it then? Well, aside from Cliff fessing up to making the call, thereby adding naïveté to the pile of horror scenarios, we have arrived, in spite of a scare curve that felt increasingly more real, at a bunch of movie clichés.

But hang on. Buried in there was a tiny scene that seemed at the time there merely to supply creep effect. A talkative stranger who approached Joey early on appears on the news program Dawson and Joey are watching at the end of the episode. He is the serial killer. Now *that's* scary.

111 — BEAUTY CONTEST (FORMERLY PRETTY WOMAN)

Written by Dana Baratta
Directed by Arvin Brown
Originally aired May 12, 1998

Guest starring: Lori Rom (Hannah Von Wedding),
Cara Stoner (Roberta Crump)

OK kids, here's the question: are we born with the instinct to fall in love, or is it constructed for us by the culture in which we grow up? Heavy questions, but enquiring Creekers want to know. Dawson thinks it has to be innate: we fall in love because we are designed to have strong and beautiful feelings for another person. Joey thinks love is something we are trained to experience, a fiction that facilitates the desires of a greater community. In other words, we are told that love is grand and ask blindly, "Where do I sign?" These kids are never going to get together at this rate. Is it merely a gender difference? Well if it is, let's mix some gender in a blender and see what it looks like.

Pacey, is that you? Our snail-boy rebel is back with a plan. This time, as Capeside is preparing for the Windjammer Beauty Contest, Pacey decides not only to introduce a prettier mollusk into the environment, but to *be* it. Pacey decides he's going to run for beauty queen and force the issue of exclusivity at its source. Are woman forced to conform to standards of beauty dictated by a gazing male, or does she arrive so eye-catching that he can't help but look? Don't look now, but Pacey's about to raise the beauty bar.

Considering that the prize of $5,000 represents liberty to a number of Capeside residents, it's no surprise that some other unlikely contestants are coming forward, namely the glamour-shy Joey Potter. Both have financial reasons — Joey is looking at higher education and Pacey wants to move out of the house — but they each become caught up in more political themes. Pacey is offended that men are excluded from the event but slips in through the technicality that there is no rule stating contestants must be women. And Joey soon realizes that there is an underlying class prejudice to the event, and finds herself suffering along the way in that she is poorer and plainer than the queen bitches for whom all pageants are designed.

Dawson, meanwhile, is stumbling around, casually insulting the self-esteem of all the girls he's loved before in a sort of anti-pageant protest, until he hears Joey sing, "On My Own." At that point he sluggishly realizes that buried somewhere in the girl he likes as a sister is the woman of his dreams. It's a somewhat spurious revelation, and Joey knows it, so when Dawson is about to bend a knee in her beautified presence, Joey pulls him up by pointing out that he has fallen for a fiction: she will go back to being Joey Potter tomorrow. The initial question about the nature and nurture of love is played out, but the answer is ambiguous. Yes, Dawson falls for Joey most when she cultivates the pose of desirability, but we already know he loves her. Did the pose merely draw out what was there? Do nature and nurture consort with the rules of attraction? Not this time, because Joey aces the whole deal with another very different romantic tradition: she just plays hard to get.

When Jen approaches Dawson in the final scene wanting him back, she is walking into a space that Joey left behind, leaving Dawson pining perfectly for the one who got away. Comb your hair back into that patented Potter do, Joey, tonight you're the object of desire.

The remaining question is, is Dawson a player or a play*thing*?

112 — DECISIONS
(FORMERLY BREAKING AWAY)

Written by Dana Baratta and Mike White
Directed by David Semel
Originally aired May 21, 1998

Guest starring: Gareth Williams (Mike Potter),
Dylan Neal (Deputy Doug Witter)

How do adults figure in dramas about teenagers? In the *Archie* comics, they are either perfectly bland or sputtering dupes; on *90210*, they tend to be marginal copies of their children, either embarrassing or ineffectual; and on *Party of Five* they are simply dead, leaving the next generation to assume their roles. On *Dawson's Creek*, the parents are full, complex characters, for the most part, if slightly less articulate than their sons and daughters. As we have seen with Dawson's parents, it is possible that the passion of adolescence survives into adulthood; however, if responsibility doesn't develop, then along with passion continue the disasters of puberty. And the effect of parents on their children's lives is profound.

In "Decisions" we see the painful source of Pacey's damaged self-esteem. His father has built his own disappointment deep into his relationship with his son. In what are painfully drawn pictures, Pacey undergoes relentless emotional lacerations as his father puts his son down in ways that are so subtle they would barely register with anybody watching. And Dawson is watching, slowly gaining insight into what goes into making a young man as troubled and intelligent as Pacey.

If Pacey is his father's biggest disappointment, then Joey's father, whose release from prison is imminent, is hers. Dawson takes Joey to confront her father, but after the long trip they arrive minutes after visiting hours, underlining another theme connecting parents and children in this episode: that there are only so many chances we are given to salvage these relationships. And in Jen's case, with her grandfather dying, time itself will run out soon enough, even for the most loving. In this scenario, as the grandfather revives long enough to say goodbye, Jen and her Grams are thrust together in their grief with the fresh awareness that sometimes it's more important that differences dissolve. As they come together to pray in church, their philosophical antagonism is temporarily swept aside. It is possible to lose those you love long before they have to go. It's a powerful message that they share, and for a time they understand that however different their means for reaching out, the end can be the same: to come together.

Meanwhile, Joey and Pacey, who have been on opposite sides of a parental blame game, also come together. Joey's desire to confront her father must be answered, and Pacey is willing to abscond with his father's car in order to get her there and, perhaps to prove his uselessness to his father. It is interesting and telling that even when Pacey is baiting the world with his recklessness, he does so in support of a higher order of responsibility.

The encounter in the prison is a fascinating one, where emotions are discovered indirectly. Dawson is left with Joey's rejected father, who asks him to describe the daughter he's lost. In doing this man a service, Dawson discovers, even as he says it, that Joey is a person for whom he has always felt a deep love, and this love that he communicates to her father is a revelation of true feelings. In the previous episode, Dawson had been able to access his feelings for Joey and came close to expressing them, but they were triggered by the image of her as a talented beauty contestant. A similar jeopardy exists here, even if the emotion seems more grounded. Have his feelings been shaped by the moment, by the metaphor of the jailed man, and projected onto the longings of the father?

When Joey's father reveals Dawson's love to her, he does so in the context of himself and the love he has for his own wife, Joey's mother. There is a strong mix of feelings in the air here: joy, love, forgiveness, and sorrow. The problem for Joey and Dawson is that this is ultimately the emotional atmosphere of a daughter and father reconciling, not that of two confused young lovers.

There is one more piece of bad timing yet. When the grieving Jen climbs up through the Dawson's window and the two fall asleep together, they will of course be discovered by Joey. Dawson has learned something in this episode: events don't conform to emotions. Things get in the way, opportunities come and go, and people who love each other have to come together through a series of adverse conditions, or not at all. Ever. Dawson finishes the season as a compelling romantic, sweeping Capeside looking for his one true love. Dawson seizes the moment, knowing it's now or never and he — finally — kisses Joey Potter. It is a very satisfying moment, and one that has been a long time coming, but the question hangs for next season: when will we know if this is true love?

201 — THE KISS

Written by Jon Harmon Feldman
Directed by David Semel
Originally aired October 7, 1998

Guest starring: Ali Larter (Kristy)

The season opener finds us right where we left off, but as Joey and Dawson's lips unlock their relationship comes a little unhinged. It's pretty much what you expect from television's most apprehensive couple and in the aftermath of the great first kiss our crazy kids experience the same old doubts. But this is a somewhat more progressive Dawson we're dealing with and before they sink back into denying their feelings for each other, he suggests that they sleep on it and see what they think in the morning. One of the curious motifs of *Dawson's Creek* is the clarifying power of a good night's sleep, and sure enough, a toss and a turn later, Joey and Dawson affirm that they are indeed on the threshold of a . . . relationship.

After beginning with this slight hesitation, the season is then thrown hopefully forward, triggering Pacey to scout the halls of high school for his own true love. And seeing as he's a man who has tasted forbidden love and feels that experience should give him the upper hand — or at least the cream of the crop — he chooses true love in the form of Kristy the knock-out. Pacey heads out looking for this hottie in his dad's police cruiser, only to stumble on a funny little bit of sunshine named Andie. Andie is new to town and Pacey uses the opportunity to sucker her by posing as a cop.

The theme of this episode is the pursuit of true love and it's only fitting that Dawson's mother, Gale, seek out her husband with the heartfelt desire to reconcile. She attempts this by stoking the flames of their once libidinous romance, but finds that Mitch has gone cold. Cold enough, in fact, to have filed papers of divorce. It's an interesting backdrop to the teenagers' evolving relationships, and, to put a finer point on the theme, we are seeing relationships that are trying to survive by either going backward or forward.

Speaking of forward, what do you do with the awkward space after the first kiss? Why, you'd better kiss again, and do it fast. Just as Dawson and Joey are about to fall into each other's arms and do just that, in comes the keening Jen, threatening to throw everything into a sudden reverse. She is still struggling with the loss of her grandfather, and her emotional condition triggers Dawson's primal confusion about the unhappiness of others. He pulls himself out of the arms of Joey and situates himself right smack in the middle of Jen's grief. It's a classic portrait of someone who simply doesn't have enough experience to know when he's adding undue complications to an already delicate new relationship. There is no questioning his motives — Jen is in real grief — but Dawson doesn't seem to see the parallel story here: he has responded to the needs of his ex-girlfriend over his new one. And that ex will inevitably need more than friendship. When Dawson has to shun the vulnerable advances she makes toward him, he hurts her further, and leaves her feeling rejected and alone.

Threesomes are getting much lighter treatment in Pacey's case. Pacey gets his date with the cheerleader only to have her show up with a boyfriend. It seems she is full of sympathy, however, for Pacey's heart condition and he quickly twigs to the fact that he has become the object of Andie's payback joke.

Katie Holmes

It's a comical inversion of the more serious events occurring in the main plot. When he meets up with Andie later, they may not be fast friends, but Pacey sure has a sexy sparring partner in this intriguing girl who's much more than meets the eye.

Joey and Dawson put themselves back on track with a first date that has them only hold each other's hand, but tempting each other to take things a step further. They end up at the Rialto on the eve of its destruction, just in time to be interrupted again by a distraught Jen. This time when Dawson runs off to console Jen, he will return to an understanding Joey. Regardless of the ongoing distraction, Jen is, after all, a friend in need. There is a maturing process going on between our two heroes and as a payoff they eventually get their second kiss. And it's a keeper.

202 — CROSSROADS

Written by Dana Baratta
Directed by Dennis Gordon
Originally aired October 14, 1998

Guest starring: Ali Larter (Kristy)

The central theme of this episode is how to makes one's own theme central when everybody else's is so darn compelling. The Leerys, who have been fairly absorbed in their own separateness, stumble upon Joey and Dawson entwined in a way the Leerys haven't been for some time. They recover clumsily, being a little out of practice as parents, and fumble rather endearingly as lecturers on the importance of safe sex. It is a healing moment, to be put back together as parents, and they experience, in a tender way, the fact that on this level they will always be together.

Joey and Dawson are experiencing a similar sensation, one that may be similar to timeless love, but there's nothing like feeling invulnerable — especially where Dawson's concerned — to make a person do the most wanton things. It's almost as if Dawson has a devil whispering in his ear, because he certainly can't hear us yelling "No!" from the sidelines as he picks up Joey's diary. Is it vanity he's seeking to satisfy as he opens the pages? What he finds there are Joey's scathing notes about his ambitions as a filmmaker. These notes are old, of course, written when Joey was feeling scorned by Dawson, and when Dawson confronts Joey, he gains no insight, but Joey hotly and deservedly takes a strip off him.

Dawson decides to take his central problem to Pacey and discovers his miffed friend is not about to give him any air time. While Dawson had been celebrating his happy relationship by nearly destroying it, Pacey has been celebrating the birthday that his best friend forgot by failing his driver's test. It seems nobody's happy and nobody's paying much attention to anybody else. So Pacey decides he'll make a move that nobody can ignore and he throws his own birthday party. He only manages to get the attention of Andie, and that relationship has yet to graduate from deep antagonism to the high attraction for which it's bound. Pacey discovers, much like Dawson, that you can't reach in and force people to like you.

There is indeed a devil loose in this episode and it's the catty figure of newcomer Abby (who appeared in only one episode last season), who picks up our neglected Jen and helps her drink her way right back to the party-girl solution. The drunk Jen then jumps Dawson and slides even further down a dangerous slope, a slope similar to the one Pacey is traveling down, as he seals out Dawson in mid-apology and turns his back on the entire world of Capeside. But if there are new devils afoot, then there is also a new angel. Andie's brother Jack has lately come to work at the diner with Joey, and he soothes her with his quiet and sane advice, sending her off with a heart full of forgiveness to find Dawson. They eventually come to a lover's understanding, but they do so under the stormy watch of the humiliated Jen and her new nasty sidekick.

Abby is a dangerous person here because she doesn't appear to have a theme she can make central; rather, she feeds off other's. Following this my-story-versus-your-story concept, Mitch comes up with a not-so-bright solution. He proposes to his wife that their marriage might be better if it just opened up a bit. In other words, instead of making this about us, which is just too damn painful, let's make it about anybody who wants it. Bad idea, Mitch.

There are moves made to heal and new directions have been taken by the end of the episode. A real friend reveals herself to Pacey as Andie surprises him with a birthday gift. A good deal of forgiveness is getting spread around and Dawson finds himself back on Pacey's dance card and back in Joey's arms. Unfortunately, he has become the prey of the increasingly unstable Jen and Abby, her nasty new partner.

Written by Mike White
Directed by David Semel
Originally aired October 21, 1998

Guest starring: Colin Fickes (Kenny Reiling)

This is the You Can't Always Get Want You Want episode, in which our Capeside lovelies learn with varying degrees of success that you only get what you need. What Mitch needs, for instance, is a sex life. All he gets at home is the vicarious thrill of his son's burgeoning love life, and even then he can only suggest ways to cool it down. His wife however, remains a very hot topic, and as jealousy flares up again the unhappy marriage is declared officially open. This strategy is obviously way off-base. Are they looking to spice up their lives or salvage what had once been a thriving monogamy? Either way, it's never going to work, and pretty soon it's clear that the bottom line to this *progressive* approach is engendering more jealousy.

And speaking of things that are never going to work, Abby is still playing Doctor Frankenstein to Jen's monster. In another case of unwholesome guardianship, Jen is becoming Abby's proxy stalker and Dawson can run, but he cannot hide.

In fact, fate is bubbling with trickery in this episode as a hat is filled with names to be pulled in order to assign partners in a classroom project that has pairs budgeting their imaginary households. There are, of course, many combinations to choose from as we have seen. As it turns out, we have a delicious variety of the very best and the very worst pairings: Pacey and Andie (Yay!), Dawson and Jen (Oh No!), and poor little Joey Potter is our single-parent household.

Meanwhile Mitch and Gale have dipped into their own

version of a hat full of names, and are out for their first mutually exclusive night on the town. It turns out to be quite miserable, which is no surprise and, really, of no consequence, because what they want out of the evening comes much later. Both try to strut their dating prowess in front of each other, affecting a casual atmosphere, while hoping against hope to catch a glint of green in each other's eyes. It's an unhappy way to be and their relationship has become a hunt for lost love in the form of inflicted pain. They communicate now through the signals of depression.

Joey's love life is showing signs of activity as she watches Jen's flirting with Dawson go into overdrive. Before long, Jen grows desperate, barging between the pair dressed as Flopsie the She-Wolf, and becoming bolder and bolder in her bid for Dawson's attention. It is definitely the Abby School of Subtle Insinuation, but the danger for Jen is her own past as she begins to revive a part of her that once had deadly consequences. Dawson does his level best to set Jen straight, but Ms. Hotsie gets in the last word: never say never, Loverboy.

While Joey and Dawson cling together battling outside forces, the household of Pacey and Andie is waging war within. Their mildly antagonistic patter takes a turn for the worse as Pacey calls Andie a spoiled brat. Too far, young man, and it seems in this nastier climate there are things you may not be able to take back. As we will discover, however, these two may be just doing some healthy testing of a lively relationship's natural boundaries.

It is the angel Jack who takes Pacey aside, revealing some of the tempestuous life that Andie has grown up with, proving that Pacey's characterization of his feisty partner couldn't be more wrong. Pacey, a man of secret and substantial honor, goes to Andie with both an apology and a completed assignment. An aura of future romance brightens around the

two, but in this episode no good couple goes unnoticed.
Tamara has come back and she's clocking these lovebirds
pretty closely.

204 — TAMARA'S RETURN

Written by Mike White
Directed by Jesus Trevino
Originally aired October 28, 1998

Guest starring: Leann Hunley (Tamara Jacobs),
Joe Flanigan (Vince)

Dawson and Joey have a relationship cemented in deep
familiarity and personal history. They know exactly what they
love about each other and share this with a natural friendship.
Sounds perfect, doesn't it? Try introducing change, difference,
and independence and see what happens. There is no such
thing as a completed person; in fact, a human life is knowable
only in terms of growth, shift, and change. Teenage life is an
especially explosive period of discovery and learning, so now
that Joey and Dawson are together their relationship is bound
for trouble.

Especially Dawson, who seems happy to have Joey as his
very own postscript, and though he may not be conscious of
this, he is completely taking for granted that Joey's entire life
began and will end with him. Big mistake. When Joey
discovers her ability to draw, an ability that she inherited from
her dead mother, it's very clear that something vital in her is
emerging. It is an important and latent part of her identity that
requires sensitivity and support. Unfortunately, Dawson is at

his least likable here. Loutish and condescending, he seems at best to be unwilling to value Joey's desire to learn more about herself; at worst he is outright threatened. When they attend an art lecture together, Joey is utterly engaged by the subject, whereas Dawson is borderline boorish. It is a stunning difference in the two and one that quickly switches their roles as serious artist and doting admirer. One also secretly suspects that Joey's earlier diary entry where she had judged Dawson harshly as a filmmaker might have been as much a part of her being creatively keen as scorned. Whatever the underlying cracks may be psychologically, the relationship is definitely not one that can absorb surprises. So Joey is left to contemplate her artsy isolation at work in the less-than-articulate company of Andie's brother Jack, the dishwasher. Little does she know, Jack is about as a surprising a fellow as ever strode the banks of Dawson's fair creek.

If Joey and Dawson can't get their relationship out of the muck, Pacey and Andie just can't stop the good-spirited squabbling. It is a form of attraction that they both understand, though it is something of a carry-over from a public school boy-girl animosity. More in keeping with the high school form, Andie goes running to Dawson and tries as subtly as she can to wiggle out information regarding Pacey's real feelings toward her. Dawson, for his part, is happy to give Andie a green light for love. The irony here is that Dawson cannot move forward in his own relationship because it is strangled by inertia and nostalgia, and Pacey is experiencing his first mature closure on a past relationship.

Tamara is back in town, and, when spotted from a distance, Pacey is compelled to leave Andie's side to pursue her. Our first reaction is possibly that this is Pacey caving in to a temptation, but when he encounters Tamara, a very adult and passionate Pacey recognizes that this is a relationship where both people have moved on. And move on he does, returning to Andie as an unburdened man who now has access to a wider range of feelings — feelings that he communicates to this lovely young woman, delighting her and us.

Meanwhile, the Dawson-Joey ground is also shifting, but rather than gaining, these two are losing each other. Joey decides that she values both her new artistic side and the part of her that will always love Dawson, but recognizes that they are at odds. She explains to Dawson that the struggle is going on inside her and not between them, so she requires space.

The question is, who *needs* to grow: Joey, or Dawson?

205 — FULL MOON RISING

Written by Dana Baratta
Directed by David Semel
Originally aired November 4, 1998

Guest starring: Joe Flanigan (Vince),
Leann Hunley (Tamara Jacobs)

The Moon. Luna. The root of lunatic. In this particular episode, the moon in question is very full, meaning most, if not all, of our Capeside courtesans are probably going to lose track of some marbles along the way. Pacey begins promisingly enough, tempering himself appropriately, in order to ask Andie out for a date. He plays the adult well, informing Andie that he will be around to pick her up at her place. Suddenly, a dark cloud crosses her face. A mysterious reaction. There is something that Andie is hiding at home. Something big.

Dating is the happy pastime that hitches itself to dark

rides this night, so when Jen and Vincent, an older fisherman with whom she has been flirting, hook up, there is no doubt that Abby, the little devil who had been pointedly overlooked in the very same flirting process, will be looking for unwelcome ways to make her presence known. When Jen mistakes Abby for a friend, as she has been doing for some time now, they both erupt into a hurtful session of name calling. Abby knows all too well how to push Jen's buttons and when she wickedly taunts her with her past embarrassment, Jen defends her own honor by delivering a sound slap to Abby's cheek. Oh well, when you lie down with the devil and all that. The two split up and head off to have competing disasters.

Jen has Vincent over to her house for a little harmless passion in her room and Abby crawls up the well-traveled ladder to Dawson's bedroom for a perfect view of the smooching couple. While Abby is stewing in her voyeuristic juices, the Leerys are downstairs doing what they do best: trying not to fight in front of Dawson, then, well, fighting in front of Dawson. Dawson races off to the safety of his bedroom only to find it has been penetrated by a very bizarrely behaving Abby. With both eyes gleaming in the full moon, Abby recklessly throws herself at Dawson. It is a strange and fascinating impulse, inspired, as all things are in Dawson's room, by Abby having watched the couple through the screen as if on a film, and now, like Dawson, she's going to direct a hot one. The blonde one resists, however, and expels the she-element from his room.

Through his window and across the way, Jen isn't having this problem, in fact, quite the opposite. It seems her little bit of fun is going the way of a date rape. It's an unsettling scene, as she struggles against the aggressive Vincent. Her savior turns out to be the avenging Grams, who, after shooing the

Michelle Williams

dockside Lothario out, sets herself on Jen, confronting her on her wanton lack of self-respect. They are harsh words, containing more truth than understanding, and Jen is sent reeling from her Grams' presence.

Just as all the respective homes in Capeside appear to be teetering on the edge, Pacey shows up at Andie's and is let in by a pleasant brother into an even more pleasant household. The illusion is shattered suddenly when a frantic Andie shows up and tries to extricate Pacey from the place. This triggers Pacey's complex self-image and when he begins to feel that Andie's trying to protect her family from him, he learns the truth. Andie tells Pacey a terrible story about her family's past. It seems her brother had died, leaving her mother so grief-stricken that she now harbors the delusion that her dead son is still alive. Pacey attempts to console her, finding himself in the middle of such profound distress that he must summon, for the first time, and not the last by a long shot, a deepening well of compassion for a situation beyond his experience.

Dawson, too, is sitting in the middle, as Mitch and Gale continue to play Jump Down The Spouse's Throat in front of their only son. Dawson soon twigs to the open-marriage disaster that's collapsing all around him; thrust in a parental role, Dawson rises to anger with great gusto. We've seen this righteous side of Dawson before: it wasn't pretty then and it ain't pretty now. Soon he reduces his father to tears, and realizes in the genuine despair of the man that adults can be as confused and in as much pain as teenagers. And in the Leery household, possibly more. Dawson is humbled by his father's emotion and responds instinctively with respect.

Little does he know that the full moon is working on *everybody* tonight, and that includes his girlfriend Joey and her new friend in all things artistic, the handsome, brooding Jack. On impulse they kiss after work, but Joey runs off, back to

Dawson with her head and heart full of unsettled sensations.

It's a very troubled population that lies awake in Capeside tonight. Pain, self-doubt, guilt, and sorrow have visited them without, as far this episode goes, any easy solutions.

206 — THE DANCE

Written by Jon Harmon Feldman
Directed by Lou Antonio
Originally aired November 11, 1998

Guest starring: Joe Flanigan (Vince),
Leann Hunley (Tamara Jacobs)

One of the key ways in which *Dawson's Creek* conveys its realism is to hammer home last week's message by having everybody repeat their mistakes. Do they ever get it right? And, more importantly, if they never do, why do they keep trying? This episode is organized around that perilous teenage ritual known as the High School Dance. It is apparent right away that our gang is simply not the type to attend predictable catastrophes like this one. They are too hip, too smart, have seen far too many movies, and have logged in far too many hours in front of the television to get suckered in. It's a step beyond the "been there, done that" variety, more like a "won't be there, won't do that" T-shirt. It takes the irrepressible Andie and her baffling school spirit to drag the sullen brainiacs off to the Hop.

The last time we saw the kids officially paired up, it was sorted out by pulling names out of a hat. This time it's the slightly less arbitrary process of asking someone out a date.

Some couples are obvious: Dawson will of course take Joey, Andie will snare Pacey — the anti-dance poster boy — and, well, because it's a school dance, football star Brett will be showcased snarling at the bombshell Kristy. No surprises there; however, events over the last few episodes have left a few people dangerously single. This is a perfect opportunity to put all these wild cards out of business, and the first to go has to be the recently desperate Jen. So Jen, who is stalking Dawson, is soon paired with Jack, who has taken to kissing Joey.

It all looks good on paper, but who pays attention to dance cards anymore? One of the problems with all this symmetry is that Pacey simply will not dance, which means anybody could end up with anybody. Jack dances with Andie. Now he dances with Jen. Now Andie dances with Dawson. Uh oh, that means Jack has to dance with Joey. While Pacey watches coolly from the sidelines he forces the situation back to nothing more than a pile of names trapped in a hat. Soon Dawson picks up on the fact that his date is experiencing some friction with Jack, and the pair waltz right out of the gym! Dawson catches up, just in time to get the gist of their dalliance, and then the gang reels back into the gym, where Dawson cold-cocks Jack in the high style of all macho boys. In fact, there are twin gender clichés afoot at this particular sock hop: defiant machismo, but also a fair bit of good old-fashioned feminine connivance going on.

Poor Brett, the jock doesn't know it, but the über-bitch, Abby, has him in her sights. Add her to the rough patch he's experiencing with Kristy, and pretty soon the evil one is supporting the athlete quite happily out on the dance floor. While Abby exploits this little piece of depressed real estate, Pacey is about to act out his own bit of gender stereotyping. After establishing himself as too male to dance, it's an easy and complimentary shift over to the guy who's sensitive enough to dance with the poor rebuffed Kristy. Unfortunately, it's a little tricky explaining this to Andie, especially since she took one look and dashed for the door. Luckily, it *is*, after all, clichés that make the world go 'round, so when Pacey catches up to Andie and wins her over, she knows that it's all man she has wrapped around her. Sensitive, strong, and intelligent — a new Pacey's surfacing (but we knew that, didn't we?).

The Leerys aren't working out so well, however. Dawson, having messed up all the good male qualities his friend has exhibited, finds himself suddenly out of a relationship. Joey needs . . . space. He messed up his sensitivity opportunity with the whole artistic issue, and as far as dignity in strength goes, he pretty much blew it when he tagged Jack. Can they be just friends again? Can two people go back when they're so committed to going forward? This storyline is given a sad treatment in the previous generation of Leerys. It seems the separation is answering nobody's needs. The future looks very painful for Mitch and Gale. What they both want to do is go back in time; unfortunately, as they sorrowfully watch each other from a distance, they are facing an adult relationship that has turned suddenly, and irretrievably, into an adult abyss. Dawson's final act is resonant with the entire family's predicament; by tossing the ladder back from his window, he symbolically banishes a part of his past that has brought his present so much pain.

Written by Greg Berlanti
Directed by David Semel
Originally aired November 18, 1998

Guest starring: Jason Behr (Chris Wolfe),
Brighton Hertford (Dina Wolfe)

One of the most imaginative features of *Dawson's Creek*, as we have seen time and time again, is the weekly device for gathering all our troubled kids together. Storms, dances, detentions, school projects, bedrooms, classrooms, and film sets have all worked their specific order of things into the disordered emotional life in Capeside. In this episode it's the sudden appearance of a pop quiz that brings everybody together for an all-night study session. Schoolmate Chris invites the whole gang, and even the very off Dawson and Joey get tricked into sharing the evening together. Andie, the overcompensating keener, sets herself up as the grand dame of tutelage, but finds herself struggling to keep the group's wandering attention. Soon enough, Chris pulls out a very different kind of quiz from a magazine that focuses on the romantic habits of young people; it just so happens that he's in a room full of young people who are just dying to hear about each other's romantic habits. It turns out this is a quiz where math becomes a particularly interesting element when the answers are given. For instance, "Have you ever had sex with someone twice your age?" Well, not many have, of course, and seeing as Pacey, in a sort of reverse swagger, has been playing complimentary virgin boy to the demure Andie, imagine her surprise when it comes out that he's had some fairly advanced sex education. The number two comes up again when Joey admits to having fallen in love twice before, much to Dawson's surprise, who has been finding solace in the fact that he's the only man she's ever loved in their short lives.

Chris, meanwhile, is a sort of backhanded success story in the conquest department. While everyone is treading lightly around each other's reputation, Chris spreads himself out in the hot tub and brags to a horrified Dawson that when the bedroom light goes out, Jen and he will be changing some of their answers to the sex quiz in a pretty direct way.

If the first part of the evening is spent playing shell games with confessions, the second half is an attempt to confront each other with what has come out. Dawson warns Jen that their host is a sexual predator with her on his radar, only to be shocked that Jen intends to make sure that when Chris gets closer *she's* going to get closer. Pacey manages to work his magic on Andie again, explaining that he slept with his teacher for baldly sexual reasons and that he is being honest about this in order to truly let Andie get access to him. What a guy. What a catch. If only Dawson had something to humble him, then maybe he wouldn't be venting his righteous anger on Chris's poor little sister. There are moments when you have to wonder, how many times do we have to let Dawson be an obnoxious fool before we completely lose our patience? It's one of the interesting benefits of watching *Dawson's Creek*: the tolerance and patience that you summon in order to accept these people week after week. I often wonder if viewers are willing to be so understanding with their own relationships. It certainly is the underlying challenge that *Dawson's Creek* throws at us. Television is often vilified for exposing us to violence, depravity, and mindlessness, while being largely ignored for the innumerable programs, *Dawson's Creek* included, that make a genuine effort to find for us the best human qualities.

And it is the difficult task of being human that guides our Capeside crew at times. It isn't granted to them easily, nor are its benefits immediate or obvious. When Joey explains to Dawson that it is him whom she fell in love with twice, it doesn't mean that he has control over her. It means he is, in the greatest cliché that ever gave young love hope, to let her go.

208 — THE RELUCTANT HERO

Written by Shelley Meals and Darin Goldberg
Directed by Joe Napolitano
Originally aired November 25, 1998

Guest starring: Jason Behr (Chris Wolfe),
Todd Sheeler (Tod Bloom)

Good news in hard times can do one of two things to a person: it can brighten your dark days and provide a hope that things can be turned around, or it can sit in painful contrast to the bad luck that seems to be a permanent fixture in one's life. Dawson's current situation, as it has been evolving this season, is now far from rosy. The open marriage of his parents is a failed experiment, and Dawson's father is now asking his son to help him pack up and move out of the family home. It is a difficult twist for the young man, who impulsively perceives the troubles of those near him as somehow betrayals directed at him personally. When Mitch tries his best to recast his relationship with his son as an evolving one, Dawson cannot see it as anything but abandonment. As they fumble through these difficult changes, both are trying to adjust to new roles that neither of them really want. Jen is also fumbling in this episode, and her increasingly unstable behavior around Dawson is about to reach a terrible low. Joey is wandering around outside the relationship she put on hold with Dawson, and has decided maybe it's not space she needs but a date with Jack. As these things darken Dawson's world he receives the aforementioned good news. It seems his first film has won him an award that sends $2,500 in his direction and he asks Joey to produce his second film. It is a great boost to Dawson and, while Joey declines to produce it, he sees this as an opportunity to make for the world a love story with a happy ending. It is, of course, the happy ending he wants for himself, in spite of the odds being currently against him. One of this episode's themes — perhaps the entire season's theme — is how do you fulfil your dreams when you have to play by the cold rules of realism?

Pacey must also contend with a bit of realism when he is told point blank by a guidance counselor that he is facing a life of wasted potential if he doesn't pull up his socks. With Andie as his bright angel, Pacey decides to turn things around, proving not only to his girlfriend, but to the viewers who have been consistently impressed by his integrity, that a focused Pacey is a formidable force of good. However, there are profound peripheral problems to contend with in this brave new world, as Andie's mother has a heartbreaking relapse into mad grief, drawing Pacey close to the center of the complicated burdens the McPhees face. Brother Jack is spending a contemplative date with Joey, as they watch far-off lightning, not knowing that this ominous sign is coming closer and nothing for them is what it seems. With Jack preoccupied with the mysteries of dating, Pacey finds himself fully entrenched in the strange battle for the sanity of Andie's mother.

If there are storms brewing at the McPhees', then for Jen they are raging. She invites Dawson to a wild drinking party,

Michelle Williams at Rock & Jock Baseball '98.

resulting in the young Frank Capra of happy endings playing anthropologist to a house full of bad actors and drunken disasters. Dawson is growing more and more intensely concerned for the out-of-control Jen, and when he goes to find her, he discovers her about to indulge in fairly shocking ménage à trois with the creepy duo of Chris and Todd. Dawson breaks up the shenanigans, but Jen, far from being grateful, is bitter that she hasn't been allowed to taste the humiliation she believes she deserves. It is an interesting playing-out of the realism theme. Jen has been acting out what she believes is a truly realistic auto-biography, grim and gritty, full of hard truths and self-fulfillment. Dawson, on the other hand, has been floating above his disastrous romantic life and dark domestic situation, seeking to attach a bright, hopeful ending to a film he wishes to base on all this. He may seem ill-equipped to deal with the way the chips are falling, but when he extracts Jen from the situation, there is no doubt that he is the one who knows the significance of what he sees. It is Dawson who has seen the dismal fiction that can result when one becomes addicted to certain ideas about realism. When he brings Jen to his father's apartment, Dawson bestows a default validity to a situation he couldn't accept. It is Dawson experiencing — and not resisting — that his life provides him with what he needs, not necessarily what he wants.

The figure of Mrs. McPhee is certainly a powerful cautionary warning about how potent the struggle between fantasy and reality can become. When she breaks down in a store and Andie is summoned to sort it out, it proves too much for the young girl. As Pacey steps in and elegantly leads the distraught woman from the store, it is Andie as much as Pacey who evolves in this scene. It is obvious that included in Pacey's emerging gifts are a surprising gentleness and instinctive sensitivity, but Andie too is learning that part of responsibility is a willingness to reach out and accept the help of others.

The episode ends with Joey returning to Dawson's empty room, and it's the picture of a lost young woman and a reminder that while the daunting landscape of adulthood is opening up, some will need to return from time to time to quiet places of childhood. Sometimes, growing up just seems like a bad idea.

209 — THE ELECTION

Written by Shelley Meals and Darin Goldberg
Directed by Patrick Norris
Originally aired December 16, 1998

Guest starring: Jason Behr (Chris Wolfe),
Colin Fickes (Kenny Reiling)

Now that we have stuffed the closets of Capeside with a ghostly cast of skeletons, it might be a whole lot of fun to see what would happen if they were all paraded out at once. In America, there's one way of guaranteeing that this will happen: politics. It's election time at Capeside High! The first team is our very own Andie, Joey, and Pacey; the second will have to be the unscrupulous Abby and her wind-up running mate, Chris. It is a great Capra-esque story, with one side having all the good intentions while sitting on all the problems, and opponents who care only for themselves and want to ensure that the good people are judged unfairly. After all, we have one mentally ill mother, one jailed father, and several sex encounters with a teacher just waiting to be exploited by the evil team.

While good people with dark secrets are trying to change the world, Dawson has enlisted Jen in a quest to earn a few stripes on the wrong side of the tracks. Dawson has been convinced by Jen that the flaw in his art is his own lack of experience with wildness and adversity. It's a comical approach, one that overlooks the fact that he just pulled one ex-girlfriend out of a drunken orgy, while the other is grappling with a sad shadow of a disturbed boyfriend. Not to mention that he has just witnessed his recently separated father and mother buffing the furniture with each other like sex machines. It seems unlikely that getting Dawson to steal a candy bar is going to gain him any useful credibility on the dark side of human nature. It is telling that Jen's forays into a criminal world are frivolous and light compared to what presents itself naturally to people every day. The dark side is, perhaps, what Jen is seeking to avoid. It is fun that she seeks really, mindless fun, which isn't in and of itself a bad thing, so when Dawson attempts to kiss her, she stops him, reminded of what it is she wants to avoid: real adult contact. There are many ways to get to the human contact you crave, but on *Dawson's Creek* there are very few that you will accept.

Meanwhile, the election is rocketing forward, and of course, with Abby at the mike, it's only a matter of time before our candidate and her team are drummed out of business, shamed by the wagging tongue of the she-devil. But our team has a trick or two up its sleeve, and if secrets are coming out, then, as Pacey gets the unsuspecting Abby to reveal over a mike she doesn't know is on, so should secret motives. Abby reveals her cynical mandate, her general hatred for the student body and, in a classic pull-back-the-curtain-on-the-wizard move, Pacey gets the front-running witch bounced out of the Emerald forest. If that trick worked once, then why not get it to work again, this time revealing the gold-hearted angel that is Andie for who she really is. It doesn't get her elected — so foul has the process been that the only survivor can be a third — and Kenny the Clean walks away with a victory.

The episode closes with everyone still sitting on time bombs. Mitch and Gale are going ahead with a divorce despite their obvious passion for each other. Dawson is bent out of shape wondering if he should be an emotional being or an intellectual one. And Andie is struggling with a medication to keep the specter of her mother from compromising her own sanity.

Many, many things can go wrong now. Think they will?

210 — HIGH–RISK BEHAVIOR

Written by Jenny Bicks
Directed by James Whitmore Jr.
Originally aired January 13, 1999

Guest starring: Jason Behr (Chris Wolfe),
John Bennes (Pharmacist)

Since so much of the season has been drawn along a conflict between fantasy and realism, it's about time we took a look at how these two concepts get hardwired. That is, how much does the life we lead owe to the art we make, and vice versa? Dawson has his new script ready, but Jen complains that kids just don't speak the way Dawson writes them, with mouths crammed full of syllables and heads stuffed with socio-philosophical constructs. It's a humorous and tongue-in-cheek observation, given that the creators of *Dawson's Creek* have suffered the same criticism. The other problem, according to Jen, is that the lovers in the movie never get to have sex.

However, the couple portrayed are based on Joey and Dawson, and it's possible that Dawson wishes to write the innocence of that relationship as a kind of unexpected ideal about teenage romance. It is either his lack of experience that limits him or a desire to paint his incomplete relationship with Joey as somehow perfect.

Pacey, meanwhile, is attempting to cash in some of his new stock as a responsible young adult to get a brand new sexual relationship brewing with him and Andie. It's not a relapse, however, as Pacey continues to play the responsibility card, getting an HIV test and laying the groundwork for meaningful contexts that might just naturally and romantically evolve into steamy heat. It is, in a sense, a kind of scriptwriting that Pacey is doing, casting himself as Mr. Right, but in the end it's obvious that Andie, while charmed by his project, is a starlet whom Pacey doesn't want to rush. It seems Pacey can't help but grow up faster than he wants.

Joey is playing out her romantic reality in the stark world of life-drawing. When she shows Jake a drawing she has done of a nude male model, the appreciative Jack promptly spills his coffee all over the well-rendered form. In a bid to make amends, Jack winds up fully peeled and sprawled across the couch while Joey shyly draws him. It is a moment that they are playing maturely, as artist and model, caught in the timeless act of drawing the nude. To break the tension, Jack describes his first sexual encounter, but as he spins his tale, an increasingly excited piece of realism pops up in the middle of this austere scene and takes them both by surprise. It seems that another timeless tradition is about to be played out, and it is somewhat less recorded in art history classes. Soon, the reclothed Jack and trembling Joey are deep in embrace and passionate lip lock. The platonic relationship between model and artist are but a prelude to teenage lust.

While most couples in this episode are including heavy

doses of self-examination with their headlong desires, it's Dawson who has somehow extracted himself from the process in order to purify experimentation. The next thing you know he's leapt into bed with Jen. Is this really what you should be doing, my boy?

211 — SEX, SHE WROTE

Written by Mike White and Greg Berlanti
Directed by Nick Marck
Originally aired January 20, 1999

Guest starring: Jason Behr (Chris Wolfe),
Edmund Kearney (Mr. Peterson)

There are lots of juicy questions that have been left unanswered when this episode begins. The scene is set when the teacher, Mr. Peterson, having just given Dawson a top grade for a mystery video project, falls upon the delinquent Abby, informing her that her assignment is due by the end of the week or she will fail. The episode's question and the answer to Abby's dilemma comes in the form of a mash note Chris finds on the classroom floor, wherein someone in the class has written quite breathlessly about a recent carnal experience. It's going to be Abby's video mystery to solve and of course, it will serve us nicely to get at the truth. The episode is thus set up as an intriguing Agatha Christie kind of mystery. Our suspects are: Joey and Jack, Dawson and Jen, Andie and Pacey. After doing some investigating, Abby uses trickery to get handwriting samples from each of the suspects, and when she has satisfied herself that she knows who has done the deed, she calls them all to a mysterious meeting at night, in Mr. Peterson's classroom. There is a great deal of resistance to Abby when it becomes apparent that she has been manipulating them all to such despicable ends. But there is so much riding on the outcome of the mystery that the participants can't help but exploit Abby's little performance to their own advantage. Dawson has seen Joey's nude drawing of Jack, so he thinks now is a perfect opportunity to ask her if she is sleeping with him. And it also gives Joey the opportunity to ask Dawson if he has been sleeping with Jen. To our great surprise they both *admit* to having the sex that the other has accused them of. As it turns out, you and I aren't the most surprised. Not by a long shot. It seems this is also news to their alleged paramours, and Jack and Jen step in to deny the act. Abby is evilly pleased to announce that she does, in fact, know exactly who wrote the note and she reveals Pacey and Andie to be the lovers in question. This is surprising, and in the ensuing argument that Pacey and Andie have, it's almost possible to overlook the scene's real question: why were Joey and Dawson lying?

Andie and Pacey have a great deal to sort out in the aftermath, including the grade that Pacey is keeping from her. It turns out that they have been feeling much the same thing: fear in the face of profound feelings. Pacey has been terrified that he will let her down, and Andie has been worried that she will scare him off. The grade that Pacey finally reveals — an A — is a sign that together they are a very good thing.

Joey and Dawson, meanwhile, take their lying to be a sign that they are still more important to each other than anyone else in their lives. Without plunging into anything, they decide mutually that their friendship is just too valuable to give up to impulses.

Dear Abby: The whole video thing, however clever, is a

clear sign that you are a bitch. This is the moment when Abby is officially indoctrinated into the Complicated Teen Club: she takes the fail rather than embarrass her "friends." Much like Pacey, Joey, Jen, and Dawson have done in the past, Abby has let her intelligence race ahead of her conscience and, like the others, she now suffers in order to do the right thing. It is an important side of Abby that will allow us a more complex view of this interesting character. And as it turns out, once everyone has calmed down, Joey and Dawson obviously still have each other foremost on their minds.

212 — UNCHARTED WATERS

Written by Dana Baratta and Mike White
Directed by Scott Paulin
Originally aired January 27, 1999

Guest starring: John Finn (Sheriff John Witter)

Time to check in on all things parental, just to get a further glimpse into the formative influences on our heroes. A fishing trip is the perfect opportunity for just such a display as Dawson, Mitch, Pacey, and his father John walk the gangplank to board the boat of patriarchal verities. We have been exposed to much of Dawson and Mitch's conflict, so it comes as a bit of a surprise when they are overshadowed by the striking dysfunctional father-son team of Pacey and John. Pacey's father compulsively degrades his son, while shining largely unwanted approval onto Dawson's shoulders. It is a dreadful portrait of a man so consumed by bitterness and personal disappointment that he systematically engenders his son with self-loathing. That Jack has also been invited on this trip, much to Dawson's dismay, is hardly enough antagonism to matter beside the colossal disaster that is the captain and his increasingly sullen first mate. It is one of those episodes that telegraphs explicitly that all problems are not created equal.

At home, Gale has gathered the girls for a work project involving the lifestyles of young women who are trying to overcome a series of generational obstacles. Meanwhile, the girls have found a secret tape in Dawson's room that pretty much puts to rest any idea that ole blue eyes isn't trudging through the randy years with the same burden as everybody else. Gale interrupts the porno and finds herself the object of one of Abby's patented ugly moments; before long, the brat is summarily evicted from girls' night.

The smaller group creates an opportunity for Jen and Joey to interrogate each other on the ongoing impossibility of their friendship, resulting in Joey confessing her deep jealousies toward Jen. It is possible that, even against the most adverse of backdrops, the kids might be doing it for themselves.

Take the fishing buddies, for instance. When Dawson can't understand Pacey's attitude toward him, it's Jack who makes clear that it has everything to do with Pacey's father's pointedly favorable attitude toward Dawson. When Pacey catches the prize fish, and it appears that his father will *have* to appreciate his son, he does, congratulating him for the one thing — the only thing, it seems — he will ever do that counts. It's a blow so explicit and graphic that it not only crushes Pacey, but pretty much knocks the wind out of Dawson as well. Dawson understands fully now, and feels for his friend, assuring him that his father isn't the last word on the worth of Pacey. It is a desolate picture we are left with regarding this crushed son and callous father, as a drunk John passes out on the beach to sound of his son's sobbing.

Equally poignant is the sight of Abby alone, unable to go home, spending the entire night on the Leery porch. There is no question that she is a difficult person to like, but as she offers Andie a ride home with the family that alienates her with its perfection, it is clear that we are being challenged to see Abby, too, as a complete person.

213 — HIS LEADING LADY

Written by Shelley Meals and Darin Goldberg
Directed by David Semel
Originally aired February 3, 1999

Guest starring: Rachel Leigh Cook (Devon),
Jason Behr (Chris Wolfe), Eddie Mills (Ty Hicks)

We've seen it here before: it's called putting out fire with gasoline. Now that Dawson has Joey back in his orbit and the two are experimenting with the delicate balance of their friendship, Dawson decides what will *really* help is going out to get another Joey. It's time to cast his film, and with producer Jen at his side, Dawson has opened up auditions looking for that elusive actor who can correctly play the elusive Joey. As it turns out, many are called but few are chosen. In a scene that is constructed out of a visual pun, Dawson stumbles onto the woman whom he thinks will make the perfect Joey when he interrupts Joey's life-drawing class and gets an eyeful of the female nude model. Devon turns out to be perfect for the role: edgy enough to make criticisms and diligent enough to follow Joey around and ape the poor girl's every move. Soon we have everybody involved, including Pacey, who learns the specifics of an increasingly unstable Andie's anti-depressant medication. Pacey responds with a flurry of concern for his girlfriend, but he is getting it all wrong. Andie has recently discarded her medication and as her mental state becomes more and more chaotic, Pacey's concern becomes the element she can cope with the least.

Joey, meanwhile, is attempting to hold up perfectly well in the bizarre presence of Devon the Doppelgänger, but when the actors question some of the emotions that Dawson has downplayed in his script, Devon takes method acting to a new level. She makes explicit that the dalliance described in the script is Joey's own, and gets a good deal of real anger to work with from her real-life counterpart. As Joey goes ballistic, the thespians go "A-ha!"

While normal emotions are being examined in front of the camera, one of the less happy managers is about to display a fairly exotic range of feeling. Andie is having trouble with a missing prop and, shaking in a manic fury, she targets Pacey as the source of all of her problems. Devon and Chris, who are playing Dawson and Joey, benefit from the real emotions they've tapped, allowing them to perform with a tremendous edge. It is an edge that also allows Dawson and Joey to confront their real feelings. They are both still very much in the spell of romantic feeling for each other, not knowing what to do, but at least they now know where they stand. "His Leading Lady" is a creative episode that reverses many ideas about how feelings are accessed. It has occurred elsewhere in the series, but never more explicitly as here, that true feelings are found by experimenting with them, and they are sometimes no more real than when they are acted out. It is not a statement against the authenticity of human emotions, but a delicate look at the levels at which they become known. Often the most instinctive feelings are there to compensate for ones which are not understood. In order to access them in ourselves, sometimes it's better to see them reflected in others.

214 — TO BE OR NOT TO BE . . .

Written by Greg Berlanti
Directed by Sandy Smolan
Originally aired February 10, 1999

AND

215 — . . . THAT IS THE QUESTION

Written by Kevin Williamson and Greg Berlanti
Directed by Greg Prange
Originally aired February 17, 1999

Guest starring: Edmund Kearney (Mr. Peterson),
Eddie Mills (Ty Hicks), Irene Ziegler (Jane Markley),
David Dukes (Mr. McPhee)

This two-part episode has to be one of the most riveting of the season. Mr. Peterson is a nasty composite of every monstrous high-school teacher who ever took his private frustrations out on a class. He catches Pacey whispering to Jack and forces the latter to stand in front of the class and read his poem. As if that weren't bad enough, it turns out that the poem is a painful series of dream impressions Jack has had of another man. This is obviously an intimate poem (and not the kindest of environments) and to make matters worse, Jack spins out of the class with tears in his eyes. High school is a tough place for just about everybody, but a kid who cries while reading an ambiguous poem about an imaginary boy is going to pretty much mono-polize both the gauntlet and the rumor mill for a good long while. Which is precisely what happens.

Speculation, much of it cruel, about Jack's sexuality spreads quickly through the halls, much to the dismay of Joey, who feels the rumors place her in awkward position. As it turns out, even Dawson feels there are some questions unanswered, but when he suggests Joey ask them, the troubled girl shuts him out, accusing him of the same nastiness as the homophobes in the hallway. Dawson has made a point, however, and both the poem and Jack linger as mysteries.

Homophobia is always ugly, but like all prejudicial fears, it can come from surprising quarters. Jen has been seeing a boy named Ty, who is an interesting and complex figure. Though a practicing Christian, he is also a full believer in satisfying natural curiosities and being open to as wide a range of experiences as he can. It is a shock to Jen therefore, when he chimes in on a discussion with a hateful anti-gay rant. It's perhaps less of a surprise that Grams doesn't disagree with him, but the disappointment Jen feels in these two people that she cares about is palpable.

Meanwhile, the situation around Jack at school is getting predictably worse as he finds his poem plastered all over. In class Mr. Peterson continues his abuse of Jack by trying to force him to finish the poem. Pacey, who has privately assumed guilt for the whole affair, rises to the challenge. He is perhaps misguided and rescuing a friend whose problem he doesn't quite understand, but when Pacey hauls off and spits into Mr. Peterson's face, we feel a strange mixture of revulsion and pride toward the purity of Pacey's sense of duty. Of course, this is an old pattern for Pacey, and it throws him right back into the delinquent bin, a bin he has just left.

Pacey is asked to apologize to Mr. Peterson as the issue becomes more and more loaded. As both Pacey and Jack feel responsible for each other's predicament, their relationship begins teetering on the edge of angry resentment.

In an impulsive gesture Joey moves in on Jack, kissing him wildly in front of his vandalized locker and the entire student body. It's not clear whom she's proving what to here, whether it's she, Jack, or the student body that has to be convinced of her boyfriend's heterosexuality. Suddenly, in the middle of this confusion, when nobody is certain where the other stands, Andie and Jack's absent father returns for a visit. They have an uncomfortable dinner, particularly uncomfortable for Jack, who sits silently, but it is oddly painful to watch Andie babble on nervously about anything that comes into her head. When they get home, the issue of Jack's sexuality surfaces, and as if to draw the matter to an acute antagonism, Jack taunts his callous father with the fact that, yes, after all, he *is* gay.

Andie is somewhat taken aback, but she seems completely capable of rallying to his defense. And when Joey is told, she too, is quietly shocked. The episode ends with Joey sobbing on Dawson's chest. There are many complex issues in the air at this point. While Ty and Grams are portrayed as religious and homophobic it is unpleasant, yet at least their position is clear. That Jack coming out to his friends and family is something of a crisis reveals much about the isolation young gays feel at the hands of those whom they love the most. It is a moving portrayal, and one that is not afraid to rid the room of heroes. Except Pacey of course, whose heroism, while endearing, is about as welcome as a pop quiz from Mr. Peterson himself.

Written by Heidi Ferrer
Directed by David Semel
Originally aired March 3, 1999

Guest starring: Eddie Mills (Ty Hicks), Emilie Jacobs (Kelly),
Gina Stewart (waitress)

Of all the "Just Say No" and anti-drinking campaigns launched every year against teenagers to deter them from putting bad things in their body, nothing compares to the sight of Dawson Leery after a few drinks. This is Dawson's sixteenth birthday and there are plans afoot to throw him a surprise party. In the tradition of all surprises, Andie, Pacey, and Joey take him out as a distraction to a blues bar that Jen's Ty happens to frequent. Once there, Andie, who is experimenting with less obsessive behavior, gets a waitress to spike the gang's drinks. Before long the loosened-up Andie has Dawson onstage to do what teenagers rarely get to do (but it seems have a natural understanding for) and that is singing the blues. This is the cute stage of teenage drinking; it's later that we get the inevitable horror story.

While this group is teething on the scenery, preparing for the chewing they will do later, all the party people are getting ready over at the Leery household. Ty, the cool Christian homo-phobe, is frustrating Jen by keeping them both in the shallow end of foreplay, and Abby is upstairs treating the freshly outed Jack like a fascinating specimen. She attempts to put him in her sexual universe by stating that everyone has varying degrees of bisexuality. It is cunning ploy that gets her closer to the young man by finding his vulnerability. Abby has described a world, a false world, where homosexuality is a kind of fiction made out of natural bisexuality. It is an attractive construct to Jack at this point — he has yet to feel an enthusiasm about his sexuality — and it presents the possibility that heterosexuality can be restored by simply calling it by another name.

Meanwhile the teenage Dean Martins are back and stinking up the joint with some fairly flammable breath. It is obvious to everybody that there has been some indulgence thrown into the effort of keeping Dawson away from the house. Joey steers Dawson up to this room, only to stumble upon Abby's experiment with Jack. Much to Joey's shock and dismay, her gay ex is smooching with none other than Abby, the Blair Witch herself. Joey flees, of course, and Dawson, who is a little blind at this point, starts laughing his head off. Soon he's back downstairs and his mood is about to turn a very drunken shade of ugly. No one is spared in Dawson's room-wide vitriol, as he lines up the people in his life, and gives his most brutal, self-serving assessment of their worth. If it is a scene through which the creators wish to convey the problems of teenage drinking, it's a very effective one. Typically in these campaigns, teenagers are depicted getting into legal trouble, going too far, and acting wild, but when you get right down to it, doesn't that pretty much sum up an ideal adolescence? No, this scene is an effective deterrent, because we know that what puts Dawson in peril with himself is to lose control emotionally: a deep embarrassment that is a matter of public record. It is definitely one of the least attractive portrayals of underage drunkenness ever conceived.

As if in counterpoint to Dawson's excess, Ty explains to his gal that his restraint has to do with a fear of being sullied by Jen, whose reputation unnerves him. He tries to be understanding, but reveals himself as a condescending and judgmental person, someone whom Jen is soon rid of. Abby,

on the other hand, is quite excited that she's corrupted
Capeside's only gay teenager, and God only knows how she
expects to get approval for this, but she certainly gets
attention: all of it negative. Jack has some explaining to do to
Joey, and he manages to do so because of the intense honesty
that has marked their short relationship.

As Dawson cools his head on the porcelain of the toilet
for the final stage of his sweet sixteen, there's not much left but
the cleaning up. Joey assures him that people will forgive him,
and that he is loved. And of course, that they love each other.
A long journey is over, many variations on the theme of excess
and corruption have been played out, and the deeper you go
into this night, the closer you get to the morning.

217 — PSYCHIC FRIENDS

Written by Dana Baratta
Directed by Patrick Norris
Originally aired March 10, 1999

Guest starring: Mädchen Amick (Nicole Kennedy),
Rachel Leigh Cook (Devon), Nick Stabile (Colin Manchester)

One of the ways we've seen teenagers work through difficult
feelings on *Dawson's Creek* has been by reflection. In art, in
acting, and in scripted moments, our heroes have found
themselves able to get closer to their strong emotions without
feeling in danger. In this episode, reflection is given a new
realm in the mysteries of the unconscious. It starts,
appropriately, in a fairly conventional dream of Dawson's,
where he is replaced both romantically and artistically by Jack.

It isn't a very likely scenario, but it allows Dawson to see his fears without them coming true. He emerges more convinced than ever that what really matters to him is his identity as a filmmaker. As luck would have it, the new teacher at school is a filmmaker herself, and, Dawson believes, the real thing, someone whom he was meant to contact. Dreams and fortune are in the air at Capeside, as Joey displays her photographs much to the interest of a very sexy professional photographer, who is particularly taken by Ms. Potter's physical charms. This magical atmosphere is grounded in the fair, where a psychic, Madame Zenovich, has opened her tent to all who wish to know their futures. Joey, for instance, has discovered that a tall, dark stranger is in her future, adding to the mystery of the attractive photographer. Madame Zenovich is an ambiguous force here, appearing every bit the sham, but capable of easily hitting the nail on the head.

Andie, for instance, is given a dark and disturbing picture of her future, which prompts Pacey to confront the seer on her craft. Pacey, who is nobody's fool but his own, wonders why Zenovich, who provides an entertainment, would want to instill fear in a susceptible person. Just as Pacey has about crushed her credibility, the psychic responds by giving Pacey an eerily accurate picture of his own situation. The thrill of this episode is held by its own unwillingness to clarify the abilities of Madame Zenovich. It is the world of weird tales, where she is both a con artist and a strange woman possessed by the beyond.

In his relationship with Mrs. Kennedy, Dawson has perhaps conned himself, but he is about to discover that the world of a filmmaker, far from being a world where dreams come true, can actually be a coldly critical place. When Dawson asks Mrs. Kennedy to give him feedback on his film, she spares no punches, perhaps going a little too far in her criticism, more as a lesson about the reality of the film industry than an informal session of constructive feedback. The two locations — the psychic tent and the screening room — are played off each other, and they cleverly rhyme each other's themes. Joey discovers that her photographer hunk is more interested in Jack; the man whom she had thought was her tall, dark stranger is meant for someone else. Similarly, the person whom Dawson had believed was fated to give him great opportunity and fortune turns out to be the most deflating personality he has ever encountered. And, to make matters worse, as she hops into Mitch's car, it seems Dawson's father was the ultimate tall, dark stranger all along. This episode cleverly conveys a mysterious sense that somehow a force of coincidences and chance is governing events, and that if you were given access to the secret code of events, prophesy would indeed be possible. But access is not possible, so when Joey exploits her discovery that Colin, the photographer, is attracted to Jack, she believes herself to be an agent of fortune when she sets them up together. Of course, one of the countervailing forces in any fortune teller's deck is the presence of a wild card. Jack is simply not interested or ready to begin dating.

As the episode draws to a close, predictability is given a fairly rough ride, an interesting element to engender in a genre of television that often sells itself on predictable mock twists. Things will have to move forward without magic wands, or idealized scripts, or snappy love quizzes, or spin-the-bottle solutions. But wait a second! Who is that figure that Joey sees through the mist as she floats down the river? He's dark. He's tall. Could it be that Madame Zenovich was the one, after all, who held all the cards? Is he handsome? Joey's heart is pounding as she positions herself to get a closer look. Suddenly the real world stabs her, as it always does, and she hovers at the end of the episode near a man who will not take her away, but will inevitably lead her back to herself. The tall, dark stranger is her father.

218 — A PERFECT WEDDING

Written by Mike White
Directed by Greg Prange
Originally aired April 28, 1999

Guest starring: Gareth Williams (Mike Potter),
Mädchen Amick (Nicole Kennedy)

There is a question common to the themes of *Dawson's Creek*, to the conflicts and vicissitudes of its characters, and it is, what is it that we do so wrong that it makes us so unhappy? It is a valuable question and one where the answer is very elusive. But more than this, it is perhaps an irrational question, even an arrogant one, for how certain can anyone be — outside of their own desire — that happiness is something for which we are responsible? It is an equation that we see fall apart time and time again in the struggles of Dawson and his friends as they experiment with their own behavior — be more like yourself, be less like yourself — with one goal in mind: to enjoy being yourself. Are these things controllable? Predictable? Or does the chaos of unpredictable influences contribute to how we feel? More importantly, are we unhappy because we are doing something wrong?

The answer, according to this episode, is plural — most defiantly yes, and most certainly no. Or in the words of Lou Reed, "Had a funny call today — someone died and someone married." The wedding in question is not one of our own, and as the elite of Capeside prepare to celebrate it, Dawson and crew position themselves in service position. The most startling position is defiantly Joey's, whose father, Mike, has been sprung from the Big House just in time to pull the Potters out of debt with a catering gig. This has Joey deeply torn, and her feelings of shame toward her father are stirred to a fever pitch. But the kids rally, as they often do in these situations, and soon we have Pacey and Andie garbing the wedding cake itself while they debate the relation-ship of this ceremony to the possibility of true love. Andie, it seems, is immovably cynical and Pacey soon recognizes that any opinion that hard and fast is probably a sign that she has buried some stronger opposing feelings. Pacey will discover, much to his delight, that Andie is, in fact, deeply sentimental about ritualized vows, white dresses, and tossed bouquets. In the course of this discovery they do, however, manage to knock the top off the wedding cake, as the ceremony lurches along in little disasters.

One of the interesting effects of rituals based in grand feeling is that they are threatened by the smaller emotions that snap throughout the day. The bride is in the bathroom weeping. It seems that her feelings for the groom may not be as grand as they should be. Dawson is outside the bathroom door, and he helps her to reconcile that one of life's important lessons involves accepting the discrepancy between how you feel and how you are supposed to feel. It's an admirable, if not ironic, opening for a hero who is burdened with his own disappointment in the people whom he loves. His father, after all, has brought the dreaded film teacher as his date to an event where Dawson's mother has confided in her son that she is determined to get back together with her husband. Meanwhile, Joey is convinced that her father is the cause of the wedding's undercurrent of disaster, and in a speech that he overhears, reveals her feelings are based thoroughly in a shame that is all her own.

True to the form of weddings, these conflicts are all sorted out on the dance floor, as couples recombine in a ritual of reconciliation. Dawson dances with his mother, and Joey with her father. As they pass each other, Joey inevitably finds herself in Dawson's arms and as they kiss, we may know that their unresolved feelings are only temporarily at bay, but to the swooning wedding guests who look on, this wedding is what it should be: destiny.

And now for the bad news. Remember the funny call Lou Reed got? Well, someone has yet to die. In the shocking and truly tragic conclusion to this episode, wedding crashers Jen and Abby have absconded with a bottle of champagne to toast their twisted alliance. The question that gets derailed in this scene is, what price will these two have to pay for the things they are doing wrong? Will they ever be liked? Will they ever find love? Will they become teenage alcoholics? The answer is breathtaking: seconds after Jen has ridiculed her for her clumsiness, Abby falls into the water and drowns. It is a cruel and swift fate that snatches her, and one that feels at its core to be wrong, to have misunderstood her; however, it is a final one. As the body bag is zipped up, a shaken Jen has been cast out of the world where people find each other out on a dance floor and into a world where people cease to be. The difference is absolute.

Written by Mike White
Directed by David Semel
Originally aired May 5, 1999

Guest starring: Gareth Williams (Mike Potter), Michelle
Scarabelli (Mrs. Morgan), Steve Boles (Minister)

Death has visited Capeside and it creates a complex whirlwind of responses. There are two profound reactions to death that are perhaps universal: One is the need to define a relationship with the person who has passed, and the other is to rekindle a relationship with others who have died. In the first order of business, Abby presents a difficult problem. She was not the most popular figure in Capeside, and when feelings of sadness begin to pour out, it is Jen, soaking in repressed feelings of guilt, who angrily blows the whistle on Andie, who has been asked by Abby's mother to deliver a eulogy.

There is a great deal of confusion here, as Jen copes in darkening ways, drinking and reeling with the resentment that she inherited from her dead friend. Andie, on the other hand, has been thrust into a position that is, perhaps, one in which she is not best suited; however, she is determined to do the right thing. But what *is* the right thing? Should the dead girl be remembered honestly, as a person motivated by her hatred of others, or should her memory be softened by forgiveness, revised by people who may really just be trying to feel better about themselves? As Jen deteriorates into self-abuse masked as a repulsion with others, Andie confronts the responsibility with which she has been challenged. Their responses are so clearly in opposition: Jen is dark, indulgent, and wrong. Andie is honest, self-sacrificing, and morally noble. The theme is not necessarily as cut-and-dry as this, however, and rests more importantly with us. It is finally to Jen that our hearts must go out, the person to whom we extend our compassion, as she drunkenly mouths her rage in church, and suffers exile from her home. We must not set Andie and Jen in opposition but, as both find themselves moving through the strange shadow world of human grief, we learn that people are never simply wrong or right: they are always in a kind of pain that resembles our own. And even if we do not like that Grams has thrown Jen out, we have learned from her that judgment is not ours, that what we do not control humbles us.

In the second order of reactions, we have the return of the dead through Andie's distressing memory of her brother, and Joey's discovery of her dead mother reflected in herself. It is an episode that presents powerful feelings in uneasy ways, so when Dawson peers over at Joey trying to detect her feelings for him, it is a relief that she kisses him, not so much because they are confirmed, but because we don't have to be subjected to Dawson's insecurities until they are absolutely, thematically necessary. Like, say, next week.

Written by Greg Berlanti
Directed by Melanie Mayron
Originally aired May 12, 1999

Guest starring: Mädchen Amick (Nicole Kennedy),
Scott Denny (Ghost of Tim McPhee)

Well, the dead are buried, and it's time to get back to the matchmaking and other shenanigans. One of the difficulties with the prime-time teen dramas and, as we've pointed out, the rest of the world, is that romantic combinations are limited by cast size, so that the same people break up only to get back together again with the same people. This is handily dealt with at the beginning of the episode as the entire cast of Capeside kids accuses itself of becoming as mired in repetition as the cast of *Beverly Hills, 90210*, resulting in a pillow fight that signals our characters will have to succumb, like the real world, to being more like a television show than they want to be.

First up is Brandon-Archie-Dawson and Kelly-Betty-Joey who believe the time has come for a little bit of spontaneity in the romance department. Dawson decides to take Joey out to a fancy restaurant to sweep her off her feet. This may be a fine idea, despite not necessarily taking us outside the realm of possibilities presented in an average *Archie* double issue, but the results, while resonant with a *90210* scenario, definitely bear the stamp of Capeside's own peculiar brand of small-world inevitabilities.

Dawson reasonably makes a reservation at the restaurant using his name Leery, not realizing that "his" table has been taken already by another Leery — his father, Mitch. Coincidence? Most definitely. Soon Dawson and Joey are sharing their romantic evening with Mitch and Nicole. This may have been a passable contrivance in a *90210* episode, but here on *Dawson's Creek*, where the real world just keeps getting realer, who should walk in for a girls' night out but Jen and Gale. Destiny or opportunity? Yes.

If this crew is experiencing some awkwardness dealing with the coincidence of each other's arrival at the same place, Pacey has taken discomfort to a new level as he tries to comprehend the arrival of someone in Andie's life who isn't even alive. The death of Abby and a variety of tensions, including the good relationship she has with Pacey, has caused Andie to relapse into the same mental illness that grips her mother. It is a dramatic portrayal of a person slipping close to the edge of madness, as she hallucinates that her brother is alive and that he is a safe refuge for her. The delusion manifests Andie's inability to accept her brother's death and apprehensiveness about trusting her feelings for Pacey. The psychological drama is played out as a stark choice that Andie must make, while locked in a bathroom. With her is the brother she lost, seemingly alive and capable of soothing her. On the other side of the door is Pacey, alive but distant, and dangerously real to her fragile, retreating sanity. She does ultimately decide to follow Pacey's voice and she comes to him with love in a scene that, while not particularly believable, is theatrically impressive. Pacey has now become a truly heroic person, almost magically so, able to steer a poor young girl from the brink of madness and draw her to him.

The forces of darkness and light, madness and sanity underscore Andie's struggle, while less consequential forces manipulate the Leery party of six. As the evening progresses Jen manages to get Gale and Mitch together on the dance floor. It seems that Gale may stay in Capeside after all, and the possibility that husband and wife may be reunited hangs over the evening. This romantic direction soon has Dawson and Joey wondering whether they might just consummate their own relationship, and while their exchange is excited with the possibility, Joey gently reminds Dawson that though it may be OK to discuss this, the time has not yet come to do anything about it.

One question remains: Why can't these people ever do what we know looks right? Can't they be trusted? Of course, Mitch ends the episode in the arms of Nicole, under the gaze of Gale. What are you doing, Mitch? Mitch? I thought we had all this worked out? Are you even listening?

221 — CH. . . CH. . . CH. . . CHANGES

Written by Dana Baratta
Directed by Lou Antonio
Originally aired May 19, 1999

Guest starring: David Dukes (Mr. McPhee)

If the problem with postmodernity is that everybody is acting like they're on TV while pretending they're not, then maybe if you stick a camera in their faces they won't be able to avoid it any longer; they'll have to start just being themselves. This is precisely what Dawson does for a film class assignment, but finds that everyone is declining. Joey certainly isn't interested and when he does manage to get Pacey to open up, the personal nature of his confession forces Dawson to shut the camera off. Where exactly does the camera belong in these people's lives? What kind of story does a camera want to tell? A good story probably, a tale of goodness. And Dawson finds

Katie at a party for her *Mademoiselle* cover.

just this sort of story in a man's transformation from jailbird to nest builder: the heartwarming confession of Joey's own homecoming father. As Dawson records this uplifting chronicle, he is forced to deal with the fact that it affects Joey, that it has real consequences. In a different version of storytelling, Joey confides that her feelings for Dawson are deep and abiding and, she adds, strangely, that all that is missing in her dream is the white picket fence. This detail seems out of place, because, while her feelings seem rooted in real things, the one thing she identifies as missing seems to transform everything she desires into a vaguely unreal dream.

The crossroads of reality and unreality that have so profoundly galvanized Pacey and Andie's feelings for each other is now facing them with separation. Andie's father has returned to take his children away, believing that his absence is responsible for both Andie's precarious mental health and Jack's homosexuality. Pacey is understandably outraged, but he underestimates the depth of Andie's fears, and the degree to which they stand between not only her and him, but her and all of Capeside. Her decision to leave with her father is mysterious to Pacey, but he loves her enough to believe that she is doing what she has to. As they kiss goodbye on the site of their first kiss, it is a deeply poignant moment, out of which Pacey emerges as a young man in the full experience of what it means to be in love.

Dawson, on the other hand, is looking, literally now, for a white picket fence. And since he sees more of the world through his camera than he does with his heart, he inevitably is drawn to Mr. Potter's world of home repair, a part of his current film project, for the object he seeks. What he finds is a startling contradiction to the story he's been telling, and, perhaps, to the one he's been living. He discovers that his subject, the redeemed man, the father of his one true love, has been lying to the camera. He has lapsed into old ways, and is probably dealing drugs again.

222 — PARENTAL DISCRETION ADVISED

Written by Greg Berlanti
Directed by Greg Prange
Originally aired May 26, 1999

*Guest starring: Gareth Williams (Mike Potter),
John Finn (Sheriff John Witter)*

Well, the season is ending and in spite of all of the more interesting goings-on, the real question is: will Dawson and Joey endure as a couple? Their relationship is certainly the backbone of the show, but as a problematic situation that must be solved it is more complicated than most. Television shows often have relationship tensions that play off our feeling of inevitability. However unsteady the couples seem to each other, as viewers we usually feel that they belong together or we simply lose interest. Dawson and Joey are different because their relationship was presented, from the very beginning, not as something they would evolve into, but rather as something they would grow out of. In episodes where they are most together, their growth seems to be suspended, and a fantastic emotion that is strong and unreal takes over. When they are either fighting or separated, they seem to be accepting the challenge of growing up. It is almost as if their relationship is like Andie's dead brother whispering to her that everything is safer in a world of make-believe.

The final episode will hang us in the place where people

either return to their old selves or grow into new ones, and

present the terrifying stakes of both directions. Joey's father is, as it turns out, dealing drugs, and with this knowledge, Dawson has to tell Joey. What ensues is an apocalypse of consequences, as the Ice House is firebombed by Mr. Potter's drug-dealing colleagues. In the middle of the fire, Jen recognizes her own all-consuming self-loathing and she waits to die in it, accepting the fire caused by another person's recklessness as her own fate. It is Dawson who positions himself as the avenging voice, accusing Mr. Potter of destroying his own family and, while he is right, this represents a relapse for Dawson, who, unlike Pacey, does not recognize when it is time for him to stand aside and let others claim their responsibilities. The series of character relapses, much like the chain of events that bring about the fire, result in sweeping resolutions from Joey, who is the season's final emotional core. And once she's made her decision, there should be no one left standing: least of all, Dawson.

THEY DON'T WANNA WAIT

Front cover: Dorothy Low/Shooting Star

Back cover: Henry McGee/Globe

Color section (in order of appearance):
Dorothy Low/Shooting Star; Lisa Rose/Globe Photos; Cleo Sullivan/Outline; Robert Hepler/Everett Collection; Greg Weiner/Shooting Star; Chris Delmas/Zuma Press; Jim Cooper/ AP Photo; Jim Cooper/AP Photo; Sam Jones/Outline; Paul Fenton/Shooting Star; Dorothy Low/Shooting Star; Terry Lilly/ Zuma Press; Dorothy Low/Shooting Star; O. Medias/Shooting Star; Barry King/Shooting Star; Lisa Rose/Globe Photos

Black and white photos in text:
7   Seth Poppel Yearbook Archives
9   Bill F. Smith/Globe Photos
11   Mark Terrill/AP Photo
15   Seth Poppel Yearbook Archives
18   Seth Poppel Yearbook Archives
23   Fitzroy Barrett/Globe Photos
25   William Plowman/AP Photo
29   Bob Greene/Everett Collection
32   Ben Mark Holzberg/Shooting Star
36   Paul Fenton/Shooting Star
40   Greg Weiner/Shooting Star
46   Seth Poppel Yearbook Archives
47   Seth Poppel Yearbook Archives
50   Seth Poppel Yearbook Archives
69   Tom Rodriguez/Globe Photos
92   Lisa Rose/Globe Photos